The Insider

CIA to the White House

Memoirs by Don Stoderl

Copyright © 2016 Don Stoderl

All Rights Reserved

Shelby Brown, Editor

To my loving wife Irene

Thank you for your encouragement and help as I put my life in writing

Some names and places have been changed or left out due to my top secret clearance and was sworn to secrecy for life.

Scripture quotations are taken from the KING JAMES VERSION

Chapter One

When I opened the letter from CIA saying that I was accepted for employment I was shocked beyond belief. I asked for the job but could a Minnesota farm boy really get a job with the Central Intelligence Agency in Washington, D.C.? I have done a lot of things and have been to a lot of places but this sounds really different and big. What am I getting myself into? As I stood there and looked at that letter I started to contemplate and reminisce on my life starting way back as far as I could remember.

Chapter Two

On a cold winter morning in 1930 I was born to a sentence of hard work for a life time. When I was about three years old my family and I woke up to discover that we had snow about five feet deep. Our farm animals and chickens had to have water to drink and food to eat. Dad, my oldest sister Martha, two brothers Bill and Leo and I had to shovel a path from the house to the barn to the water pump and finally to the chicken house. I used a small shovel that was also used to clean ashes out of our wood burning stove. Every winter day in Minnesota was very cold, however, it was never too cold and no one was too tired or hurting to work every day but Sunday. Every Sunday Mother, Dad and five children got in the old Model T Ford car and went to the Catholic Church. One day when Dad was cranking the car, it back fired and broke his arm. Then he showed my oldest brother Bill how to start it and not break his arm. It only took a few months and Bill broke his arm. After that we jacked up the rear wheel, put the car in gear and turned a rear wheel until the engine started. Our next car was a Model A Ford, a much better car and with a battery operated starter.

Our farm was one and a half miles from school. Every day we walked to school and back snow, rain or shine. I don't ever remember when a school day was cancelled for any reason. There was a public school only one half mile from our home. In that school there were only ten children but we were not allowed to go there. We were Catholic and had to go to the Catholic school. Before school we did a lot of the farm chores and after we got home we did the rest; such as gather the eggs, water and feed the cows then milk them and separate the milk from the cream. After supper we had to candle and clean the eggs. Candle means to make sure there is only one yolk and no blood in the egg. We also had to split wood for the kitchen cook stove and the stove in the living room. That was our only source of heat in our house in the winter.

We had no electricity on the farm in those days. Using kerosene lamp we would do our school home work. School was hard for me because somehow I got a bad start. There was no kindergarten in those days. When you were six years old you started first grade. It was a Catholic school and the Nun that taught first grade also taught second and third all in the same large room. Altogether there were about thirty five children in that room. She would go from one grade to the next and then back. There was no time ever to ask a question. She just could not give enough time to each child, especially if a child was a little slower than the rest. Maybe I was one of the children that was slow for some unknown reason. I got a little behind and the Nun just didn't want to help me. I don't know why. I guess her philosophy was, keep up with the rest of the class or get left behind. Fourth and fifth grade was taught in another room and sixth, seventh and eight were taught in another room. My first grade teacher told my parents that I was slow. At home my brothers and sister couldn't help because they had their own homework to do. It was always late when we started and very late when we finished. Mother and Dad were no help because Mother had a third grade education and Dad a fourth. They both had to stop school when they were young to help on their parent's farm. It didn't take but a few years and everybody started to say Donald is slow, the Black Sheep of the family and would never be anything. Even adult relatives and family friends called me a Black Sheep. I wanted to learn but the Nuns were always busy helping others and I wasn't worth helping. When I was alone I would cry because I wanted to learn. All through my young life it was that way. Sometimes instead of learning in the class room, the teacher would send me to help the House Nun with her house work. Several times I had to carry the laundry water outside that the House Nun used. I also helped the janitor cut and carry wood and coal for the school furnace. My treatment in school started to run into my treatment at home. When one of my brothers or sisters had a birthday, Mother would make a birthday cake and invite Grandma to our house. Grandma would give that child a fifty cent piece which was a lot of money in those days but when I had a birthday Grandma would sometimes be invited to come but never a cent as a gift. I don't know why but it hurt me like many other things did. It wasn't easy being a Black Sheep. It was said that Mother and Dad would have to take care of me all my life. That hurt me because I knew I was somebody, I was a person, a young sensitive child. I felt that even our farm animals were treated better than I was.

Chapter Three

As we three boys got older we started to trap wild animals in the winter and sell their pelts (skin & fur). The first animal I trapped was a skunk. It was so beautiful with those bright black and white strips down his back and face, that I did not have the heart to kill it. I stepped forward to let it out of the trap when it sprayed me right in the face and all over my clothes. I hit it with a club that I carried to kill my animals. The skunk died real fast. I had to skin it and put the pelt on a frame to dry. Next I took a bath in the near-by river where the water was ice cold and there was snow on the river bank. I then walked home with only my long winter underwear on. I was so cold that I thought I would never get warm again. At home I put on clean clothes and put my stinky clothes in a tub with water and very strong soap, lye soap. Then I walked to school and after school I washed my clothes out and hung them on the clothes line to dry. When I sold the pelt I got two dollars for it. Another time I was trapping muskrats. I set the trap in a muskrat mound. The next day I went to check my trap and I couldn't see it. With my left hand I felt in the mound. The muskrat was alive. It bit my finger and would not let loose. I pulled the muskrat out with my trap attached and tried to choke it but it would not let loose of my finger. I had to kill it with my club and almost ruined the pelt because I hit it too many times. My finger didn't hurt at the time because my hand was numb from the cold but when I got warm it really hurt. I washed it good with soap and water, tied a cloth around it and in a few days it was good again. I got two dollars for that pelt also. Every day my brothers and I learned more about trapping wild animals and how to kill them without damaging their pelt. We could tell from the tracks animals made what kind of animal it was. Very often we would follow the track of an animal to its burrow and set a trap. Most of the time we would catch that animal.

The three of us had different trap routes but sometimes we did work together and always sold our pelts together. We never thought or worried about an infection. When we got hurt, and it was often, we would make it bleed a little and keep going. We also sold horse hair, any metal and bottles we found. With that money for a start we bought more traps, ammunition and anything else we needed. We bought and sold guns, knives and everything else with our neighbors young and old. We also made things. Sometimes just toys and sometimes things that was dangerous.

Once we made a gun from parts and pieces we found around the farm. When it was finished we wanted Bill to shoot it because he was the oldest but Bill said, "no". Then Leo should shoot it. He said, "no" let Don shoot it and I said "no". If it was too dangerous for them I don't want to shoot it either. So we tied it to a tree, put a string around the trigger, stood back behind a building and pulled the trigger with the string. It went off and it blew in a thousand pieces. I knew we had good angels watching over us.

We all made and each of us carried a sling shot. We were very good shots with it. We shot birds and small animals and everything on the farm had a hole in it or a large dent. We also made bow and arrows. Some were so strong that when we would shot an arrow up in the air, we would lose sight of it for a few seconds. We always had a long nail in the end of the arrow. One day we shot an arrow in the sky, and then waited for it to come down. As it was coming down we saw that our kid sister Marie was walking across the yard and we hallowed, Run Marie! As she started to run the arrow came down and pinned the back of her shoe to the ground and she fell over. At first we thought we had killed her but she got up, picked up her shoe and continued walking to the house. It was just another day on the farm with three boys.

One Sunday afternoon we three boys were in the woods hunting when I saw a ball of fur on the ground under a big tall tree. I picked it up and it was a baby owl. At first I thought it was dead but then it moved. We wanted to keep it but knew it ate meat and our trapping season was over. Brother Bill shot a squirrel for meat to feed the owl. We took both the owl and squirrel home, cut the squirrel in little pieces and put a piece in the owl's mouth. It was so close to dead that it would not swallow. An hour later we opened the owl's mouth, looked in and the meat was gone. We put another piece in. An hour later it was gone too so we kept doing that until it got dark and time for bed. The next morning we gave it another piece and it sat up, it was getting strong. We couldn't keep this up because we had work to do plus we had to go to school. We asked our Mother to feed it while we were in school but she said no, that she didn't want an owl around to eat her chickens. On our way to school we set a couple traps for rabbits or gophers. On our way home we found that we had caught a gopher in one trap. Our owl ate the cut up gopher that evening and the next morning. He was getting stronger so that meant we needed more meat and more trapping. That went on for some months until we couldn't get enough meat for him. He was getting older, stronger and then started to fly so he started to hunt for himself. With the food he caught and the food we gave him, he was still always hungry. We looked in a bird book and found that he was a screech owl so we called him Screechy. It didn't take long for him to know his name. He grew big, strong, had big wings and big sharp claws. When he was young he would sit on our arm or shoulder but now his claws were too long and sharp so we got a stick about twelve inches long and one inch in diameter. One of us would hold that out with both hands and call him. He would come to us and land on it. He enjoyed being petted, talked to and would still eat small pieces of meat from our hand, although he enjoyed larger pieces so he could tear it apart with his claws. In the morning when we would go out of the house to start our work he would sit there so we could see what he had caught to eat. Or, was he bringing us a gift? I think he liked mice most of all. In all the time we had him, he never bothered our chickens. I guess he knew they were part of our family. He was also a good friend of our dog and cat. From the start we would talk and play with all three at the same time. As time went on he would stay away longer each time he flew off. The first time he didn't come home for a day and night we went to look for him. We walked in the woods where we found him and called his name. After a couple hours he come flying to us. We knew then he was getting older. We also knew that one day he wouldn't come back and he didn't. Maybe he found a girl friend. We hoped he did. We had him about a year and a half.

Chapter Four

The old Model T Ford was just sitting around for a few years. Dad used the frame and motor to make a big saw to cut wood for our wood burning stoves. The body of the Model T was aluminum so we three boys cut a few little pieces from it about once a month and sold it to the junk man in Wadena with our cans, bottles, pelts and anything else we had to sell. Wadena was about six miles from our farm. How did we get our things to town to sell? Every Saturday Mother and Dad would go to town to sell the milk, cream and eggs. Mother would shop and Dad would go to the beer joint. So the Saturday that they were going to town one of us boys would have everything in a sack and as they started to leave, that boy would jump on the back bumper of the Model A Ford and ride the six miles to town. As they got to town Dad had to slow down to make a sharp turn. That is when we would jump off, and go sell our stuff at the junk yard. Then walk up town to buy shells, traps and anything else we needed. After that we would walk back to the corner, hide and wait for our Mother and Dad to come to that corner again. Then we would jump on the back of the car and ride home. In the meantime the two that stayed home had to do the work of three. This trip usually took all day. The trip home was not safe because Dad always had too much to drink. I'm sure some people saw us but I guess they said it's just a Stoderl boy being a Stoderl boy. They never said anything to our parents.

Our Mother was a good hard working lady and Dad was a good manager. We always had a good home and enough to eat. Dad worked hard and long hours like all farmers.

But later as my oldest sister, my brothers and I got older Dad started doing less. Sometime later he decided to move to town and let my sister and us boys run the farm. World War II had started and a few months later my brother Bill joined the Navy and my sister got married and moved to town. My brother Leo was no farmer and left for a job in Fargo North Dakota and later he joined the Navy. Then Dad sold the farm to his brother and sister-in-law and told his brother that Donald would work for him. I worked for him for only a month because they didn't cook much and I was always hungry. They didn't have sheets for my bed plus they were always fighting and drinking too much. It was very depressing to be around them. All they wanted was a slave. For all that I got no pay, maybe Dad got it I don't know. Every Saturday and all summer Dad always had a job lined up for me with some farmer and he took the money that I earned. I never got a cent.

Chapter Five

When I was twelve I got what everyone called the seven year itch. I had it all over my body and it itched all the time. My hands were so full of blisters that I wore gloves all the time so people wouldn't see them. I kept hoping and wishing that the seven years would go fast. About a year after I got the Itch my sister got it. A week later Mother took her to the doctor and got a salve for it and within twenty four hours it was gone. A week after that my Mother took me to the doctor and got the same salve. Today I know it was scabies, a condition caused by mites as they get under the skin. A person can get it from an animal, another person or from a plant. It should be treated as soon as possible so another person doesn't get it from you. Life was not easy for a Black Sheep. I was a no-body. The only time I was somebody is when Dad got a job for me and he got the money that I earned.

Chapter Six

When I was fourteen years old I decided that if I was going to be anything in my life, I would have to do it on my own because there was no help from anyone. I hope to have a long life ahead of me and I'm not going to let anyone upset my future with words or try to hold me back. That summer I was sent to Valley City North Dakota to work on my Uncle's farm. I did the work of a man and learned a lot but Dad got the money that I earned.

When I was fifteen years old I left home in the summer and hitchhiked to North Dakota to work on a farm driving a tractor. Two weeks after I got there I wrote a letter home to let my parents know I was alright and working on a nice farm for a very nice couple. They were young, without children and could not be nicer to me. The next day Dad came and got me and the money I was owed. I never got a cent of it. I missed that nice couple and thought of them for a long time. They weren't like the people around home. They treated me as a friend and their son not as a slave or hired hand.

Chapter Seven

I went to the Catholic School another year but did no better than before because the Nuns would hardly look at me unless they wanted me to carry the laundry water outside or help the janitor. For all the years I went to that school if there was any trouble on the playground they always blamed me and the Nuns would pull my hair, my ears and hit me. One day, my last year of school a boy that had always picked on me and other kids, hit me and pushed me over. That was all I could take from him after all these years so I gave him a bloody nose and a black eye. Then the Nun gave me a beating, grabbed my hair and ear and started to shake me, then hit me across my knuckles with the edge of a ruler. When she was finished I stood up, looked her in the eye and whispered, don't ever touch me again. I was lucky she didn't or I would have spent the rest of my life in jail. When I told my Mother anything about the Nuns she would say that I should just be good. To Mother and Dad the Nuns and the Priest could do no wrong, they were like gods. Maybe I was the cause of or involved in some trouble because I was a boy and felt depressed and hurt but not all the problems or trouble. I didn't want to be the problem; I just wanted to learn with the rest of the students. To the Nuns I was no more than a stick of wood or an empty desk. They were responsible for it being said that I was slow and a black sheep. The only way to get rid of that name and be somebody was to leave the area and never come back, which I did.

Chapter Eight

The next summer I was sixteen and Dad had a farm job for me about two miles out on Highway 10. I was supposed to be at that farm at seven in the morning. As soon as I got on the highway I started to hitch-hike. I said to myself, "the Black Sheep is dead and buried", this is my life. I can do and be anything I want to be as long as I have faith in myself and a strong want to and my "WANT TO" was very strong. I had no money, washed out bib overalls, shirt and shoes that my older brother wore for a year or two. Five minutes later a car stopped and asked me how far I was going. I said to Valley City North Dakota to work for my Uncle. It was a lie but he didn't know it. It was the only city and place I knew outside of my home. He said he was going to Casselton just on this side of Valley City.

Casselton was a small farm town. I walked the streets and found the city park where I would sleep that night. At dark a couple came by and asked if I wanted to sleep on their living room carpet. I did and the next morning at six they woke me and said wash up and have breakfast with us. That would be my first meal in twenty four hours. What a nice gift they were giving me. I don't know who they were but I never forgot them. What a nice compassionate couple they were to do so must for a nobody. The next morning I got a job on a Casselton farm using a wagon and horses. I was to load grain on it and when it was full I was to drive it to the thrashing machine and unload it. There were five other men with wagons. When it was my turn to go to the thrashing machine my wagon was less than half full. I was too young, too small and too weak for that kind of work. The owner asked me if I could drive a truck. I lied again because I needed a job, a place to sleep and food to eat so I said yes. He took me to his grain truck, showed me all the gears, and told me how to load the truck with grain from the thrashing machine. He said when the truck was full to drive it to town. Go to the grain elevator, give them his name and they would tell me what to do. That job I could do. Everything on that farm was hard work because I was only a kid that weighed one hundred and twenty five pounds and thought he was a man. I didn't look back, only forward because I knew I could do anything, maybe a little slower than a full grown man but I will not give up, I will not quit.

Chapter Nine

When that job was finished I went to Moorhead Minnesota and got a job at a gas station. After a week of day work the owner sat me down and gave me some fatherly advice. He knew I was young, uneducated and alone. After a long talk he said I should go to High School and he would help where he could. He told me that he wanted to keep his gas station open at night and to help me and him he would give me the night shift. That way I could do my homework after midnight when business was slow. He took me to the School and got me started. We talked to the school counselor and a teacher and told them the trouble I had in the Catholic School. They were very understanding and said they would help me all they could. The first thing I learned was how to learn, how to study, how to memorize and to take notes. Everybody was very kind, helpful and interested in me. I would get off work at six in the morning, eat breakfast then sleep until eight thirty, dress and run to School. It was two miles and at first I would run one mile and walk one, later I could run the complete two miles and after School I would go to my room and sleep, then eat and back to work at eight pm. A very nice girl helped me with some of my school work. She wanted to come to the gas station and help with my homework but I told her there just wasn't time to do homework until after midnight. Sometimes the owner of the station would buy my breakfast and then take me to school. He was a very nice man, a big help to me and a great motivator. It was a seven day work week because I needed the money. Although I was way behind I really liked school, the teachers and all my new friends. I found that learning was fun and very interesting and I also wanted more but what I needed most was more sleep. A few times I fell asleep at work for a few minutes. One time a police man came in and woke me up. After that I was more careful to stay awake. I finished that year with flying colors because I had lots of time to study and the teachers were very nice, helpful and real motivators.

When school was out I asked the girl that helped me a lot if she would like to go with me to a movie on Saturday night. She accepted. Saturday night finally came. I walked to her house and asked her Mother & Dad if I could take their daughter to a movie. They said yes but have her home before eleven o'clock. She would be my first date and I didn't know what I should say or talk about but as it turned out we never stopped talking to each other. She lived over a mile from me but in those days everybody walked or took a bus. We walked for a while and then went to a movie. When I got her home she gave me a hug. That was the first time in my life that anyone has ever hugged me including my parents. I was so happy I felt like skipping and dancing all the way home. I cherished that evening for months. What a beautiful young lady she was. I know I'll miss her. She was an inspiration, a big help and gave me "<u>my first hug</u>".

After school I went back to the farm country and got a job driving tractor and later a truck. When School was to start I went back to Moorhead Minnesota. I got a night job in a bakery wrapping loaves of bread using a large machine. It was easy work and a nice warm place to work in the winter. I was able to get a nice room close to school. The pay in the bakery was more, the hours better and I loved the work. I had to take a bus to work because it was about three miles from my room and after work I walked and run home because the buses stopped running at midnight. My Boss was real nice and easy to work with. He and I were the only two that worked at night. Later the delivery drivers would come in to load their trucks with what we wrapped. School was fun and every day was a new day. I was learning a lot and even thought about being a doctor someday. I had no time for sports. I just wanted to study, learn and work. That year I learned to type and finished with sixty words per minute. The same girl and I became good friends again. She was a big help with my school work and in my life. She invited me to her home for dinner a couple times and we went to a movie a few times. Her Mother & Dad were always very nice and friendly to me.

I only got one night a week off and I'd rather sleep and study then go out although I enjoyed being with her. She was very affectionate and a pleasure to be with. We held hands whenever we could.

After school was out I again went to work on a farm, driving a tractor, a combine, then a truck. I worked on a farm both years because the pay was better and the room and board was free or included in the pay. After that I went west and picked potatoes. One day a man that was picking next to me took a sack of my potatoes. I told him to put it back and he just laughed at me because I was smaller than he. I beat him up pretty bad before the boss stopped us. After that the boss had me drive a truck which paid more and was easier work. What the bully didn't know is when we boys were young and still on the farm, we bought or traded for a set of boxing gloves. Dad showed us boys how to use them and said, always get in the first punch. We boxed each other and all the other boys in the area. It was said that in a fight the Stoderl boys were holy terrors. I guess we got pretty good because after some time none of the other boys wanted to box with us.

I went to Idaho to drive a potato truck and then a sugar beet truck. The boss and his wife were very nice and asked me to stay with them all winter. I said the work is finished, why do you want me to stay? They said to help service and repair equipment and help around the farm. Then they said when all the work is finished we will hunt and fish in the mountains. I wanted to go back to school but it was too late so I stayed at the farm and worked for them another year. We hunted in the mountains, shot a deer and fished in the mountain streams for trout. It was all so different for me and another great experience.

The warmth and compassion showed to me by so many nice people since I left home is beyond words. I thank God for every one of them. I didn't know there were so many nice, friendly and helpful people in the world. I also learned that there are some that are not so nice but they are in the very low minority. I enjoyed life and I believe I developed a faculty of curiosity and adventure. The more I did and saw, the more I wanted to see and do. I enjoyed traveling, maybe just to see what was over the hill.

Chapter Ten

The next winter I was in Denver Colorado. When I got there it was cold, snowing and no work plus it would be Thanksgiving in a couple days so I went to Lowry Air Force Base and joined the Army Air Corp. After a good thanksgiving meal and lots of paper work I wrote to my Mother & Dad and told them I was in the Army. That was the first time I wrote to them because now I knew that Dad could not come and get me and my money. I was sent to Fort Ord California by train for my basic training. We arrived at Fort Ord at lunch time and as we sat down with our lunch the guy next to me, who was a bully and a big mouth to everyone on the train, cut my cake in half and took half. I said put it back. He laughed at me and started eating it. I said, we are going outside and I grabbed him.

Outside we fought and after I knocked him down twice the Sergeant made us stop. The second time I thought he fell on his own so the fight would stop. After lunch the Sergeant formed platoons and made me a squad leader in the first platoon. A couple weeks later the Company Commander called me to his office. I was really scared and worried. I didn't know what I might have done to be called in. When I had gone into his office, he asked me to represent the company in a boxing match at the Military Post or Base level. He also said that if I did well I might be at this Base a long time. I wanted to please him but what I wanted more was to finish my basic training and get more education, so I declined.

It was near Christmas at that time so I sent my sister Martha money to buy our mother an electric toaster. It was something she wanted for a long time, ever since she and Dad moved to town. When she opened the box she was so happy she cried. The next Christmas my oldest sister and we three boys bought her a refrigerator. When she saw it she said, I thought I was in heaven. Our Mother deserved more than we could give her.

After basic training I asked to go to OCS (Officer Candidate School) or Photography school but was turned down because I didn't have a high school education. I was sent to the island of Adak in the Aleutian Islands. While I was on Adak I was the Dock Master and in charge of three warehouses. I had six men working under me. Everything that came from the States was unloaded from the ships and put in one of my warehouses. Then it was separated and sent to the units that requested it. At night I went to school, finished two years of high school in one year and got my GED. Hand writing notes were slow and I often missed what I wanted to remember. I wanted to learn shorthand but the subject was not taught. Years later when I would attend meetings I wished that I would have taken shorthand in college. Most of the year I was on Adak it was dark, cold, windy and wet. I was sure glad when that year was over.

Upon arriving in the States I went on leave for thirty days. It was good to see my Mother and Dad again. They were glad I was in the Army and doing well. I'm sure there were no hard feelings about me leaving home the way I did. At least it didn't show. They had moved to another town about thirty miles away so I made new friends. Met some nice girls, did a lot of dancing, drinking and partying. After being on an Island for a year with only men, I guess I got carried away with drinking and partying. It's all I wanted to do until I left for my new assignment. One girl I especially liked. She was a farm girl that liked to party. Of all the girls I met and dated while I was home, after I was gone for a month or two her name was the only one that I remembered. It was Doris, the lady that I later married. After I left for my new Military Post I started writing to her and each time I returned to Minnesota I would spend most of my time with her.

My new assignment was Fort Riley Kansas. I worked in Supply and at night I went to college and completed one year before I was reassigned. I met a nice girl student that wanted to be a teacher. She asked me if I could roller skate. I said no but I would like to learn. She said OK, every Saturday night we went roller skating at a nice Skating Rink in town.

And if you really want to learn I'll be glad to teach you how. I said OK, I'm ready to try. First just going forward was hard, then turning and going backward, then dancing. It was a lot of fun but I spent a lot of time at first against the wall and on the floor, on my butt. I enjoyed being with her but that is as far as it got because we both wanted to study and do well in school. She also had a job and paid for her own education. One evening they had special roller skating but I had to work so I sent a friend to skate with her. When he told her that he would skate with her because I had to work, she told him she would skate alone. That surprised me because we agreed that we would not get serious with each other. When I asked her about it she said she did not love me but if she could not skate and dance with me then she would do it alone. That was OK with me. She was not a party girl and I had grown out of it. It was time to settle down and think about my future. It would have been easy to love her but school came first. Plus I was writing to my Minncsota girl Doris. Doris and I talked about marriage a few times in our letters but did not set a date.

Chapter Eleven

My time in the Army was up in the winter so I got out and went to Minnesota. I bought a car and Brother Bill and I went to all the large cities trying to get a job. After two months we still had no jobs and because of the cold weather I knew I didn't want to ever live in Minnesota in the winter. We talked about going south where it is warmer but my money was fast running out and Bill had none to start with. Doris and I talked about getting married but with no job and no money I told her we would have to wait.

I went back into the Army. And again got stationed in Fort Riley Kansas and assigned to the same unit doing the same job. I also started college and finished one more year.

The Koran war started and most of my friends were sent overseas to fight. It didn't take long until I received letters from my friends saying some of the men we knew were killed and some injured. I married my Minnesota girlfriend Doris, and six months later I was transferred to Camp Crowder Missouri. Doris seemed to like military life but she still wanted to party and smoke. I no longer cared to party so we had to make that adjustment. I didn't smoke and I had stopped drinking. I had hoped that she would grow out of it fast because we just did not have the money. I asked her to get a job but she did not. She did stop drinking but she did not stop smoking.

After WWII Camp Crowder was closed and the buildings were leased to the farmers in that area. When I arrived the buildings were a mess, full of snakes and rats. The farmers used some for chicken houses, grain storage and other farm usages. I didn't think they would ever be usable for military men to live in but the Army thought different. We worked and got them fit and usable if you stretched your imagination.

My Son Clinton was born at Camp Crowder in the Military Hospital. He was a beautiful little guy and as fat and round as a pumpkin. We really loved him. He gave us a reason to live and plan our future. We had no family there but we took him all over and showed him off. He was our pride and joy. I took lots of pictures of him and sent them to our parents so they could see their beautiful Grandson.

Several months after the Base was cleaned and ready for inductees I was transfer to Washington DC. There I worked in the Pentagon and was the Supply Coordinator for the Signal Corp and Security Officer for the Signal Corp procurement office. My Mother and Dad were very proud of me, in fact so proud that they told everybody they knew and even people they didn't know that their Son worked in the Pentagon. About two years later my time in the Army was almost up so I applied for a job with CIA not really knowing what I was getting myself into. I was thinking and hoping it might be an office job in Washington, D.C. It would be something different and it sounded exciting. Then it appeared to me that those two things were part of my life, always looking for something different, something exciting. When I was accepted for the job with CIA I again got out of the Army. It took some time for my security clearance to come though so I started college again and finished one semester. During that time CIA paid me a very small living allowance so I wouldn't look for another job.

Chapter Twelve

Sometime later I received a letter from CIA that said it was time to start training to be an undercover agent. I pondered that for a moment and wondered if a Minnesota farm boy, turned soldier could actually become an undercover agent for the CIA? The letter said I should go to room number 204 at an address in down town Washington DC and report for training. When I arrived at the address given to me I could see it was not a CIA building and wondered why. There was no parking in the area so I had to walk a mile and all that time wondering, what was I getting myself into. My mind fired off one question after another. When I arrived at the building and walked through big doors, I was wondering if I should turn around and leave or run. I could get a job someplace else in town or maybe leave

Washington. Maybe go to Florida where it's warm in the winter. The elevator was on the right and the stairs on the left. I took the stairs to give myself more time to think. On the second floor, there it was; room 204. I opened the door and there sat at the reception desk, the most beautiful young lady I ever saw, and in a dress that hid little. I know my eyes were big and my mouth was open. She asked in a very sweet voice, what is your name? I told her and she made a notation in her book. Then she escorted me into a large room with about thirty five men and ten women. Only a few were talking, most were just sitting straight in bewilderment. A few minutes later a big man that looked like a Marine Corp Drill Sergeant walked on the stage. He was over six feet tall and weighed over two hundred pounds. Now I'm really wondering what I got myself into.

The meeting started and he asked how many stared at his receptionist. Everybody put their hand up. He said she is a member of our training staff. I think most men sat up a little straighter, overconfident thinking they would not be duped again. Then he said you will be taught to keep your mind on your business and never let a pretty girl distract you from your work. You will never go into a known CIA building. You will not admit you work for the CIA. You will say that you work in a classified position in room 204 of this building. And you will not trust anyone. You have now started your training to be a CIA undercover agent. Half of you will not complete the course. You will either quit or we will suggest you look for another job. Nobody moved. It was a lot to take in. But I liked everything he said. I'm going to love this job. I knew I would not fail nor quit because I have never failed or quit anything I wanted to do. I have taken detours but I have not failed to meet my goal. That was my destiny.

The training took a year and was all over the Washington DC area. Whenever the big marine sergeant showed up we knew that for the next week or a month our training was going to be hard and even dangerous. At other times it was fun, concentrated and a persuasive learning process. I knew that as soon as I got into real undercover work, life would be all work and no room for mistakes. One mistake could cost you your life. One of the many things we learned was to see and hear everything. Now, fifty years later I still see and hear everything that goes on around me. After six months our group was down to ten men and two women. The twelve of us became a close family and we all completed the course. Most of the training for the women was separate from the men. In addition to my training as an undercover agent, I also learned a language well enough to do my work.

Chapter Thirteen

There was a big party with lots of food, liquor, music and dancing. Some thought it was part of our training so we all drank only enough liquor to feel it. None of us wanted to make a fool of ourselves and be kicked out of the program. Several hours later the party stopped and the Big Sargent appeared. He said "GOOD BYE", have fun, work hard and stay alive, your training is complete and it's time to go overseas. I'll miss that big guy and my classmates, but life goes on.

My assignment was to the Far East. I asked if I could delay for a few months because my wife will have our second child in three months. They told me to bring a letter from her Doctor and they would try to delay our departure. I told them that my wife will not go to a Doctor. They said; then you are on your way overseas. I guess they didn't believe me. They didn't know my wife. I begged her to go to the Doctor but she would not go. We drove to Minnesota and two days after our arrival my wife Doris gave birth to a beautiful baby girl that we named Eunice. Since she was three months early, she weighed a little under four pounds. They kept our baby girl in the hospital incubator for two weeks and we stayed at the home of Doris' Mother & Dad's. Doris smoked so heavily, they would not let her be with or hold her baby. I went to see and talk to Eunice twice every day the first week. Only her Nurse with clean white clothes could hold and feed her. The second week they told me that I could hold and feed her if I put on a hospital gown or robe. So I went to see, visit and feed her three times a day. She was so beautiful and so very small. When she was two weeks old I took a picture of her and made an application for her passport. Clint was on his Mother's passport. The day I took little Eunice home from the Hospital I had to leave for my new assignment. Eunice was too young to travel so I went by myself and one month later Doris and our two children came. I know it was a very hard trip for her but there was nothing I could do about it. There was a large American Military Hospital in the city where our new home would be. Since I had a Department of Defense Identification card we could use the hospital for our medical needs. The day I picked up my wife and two children at the overseas airport, I took little Eunice to the hospital for a check-up before we went to our new home. The Doctor took the history of my baby, then checked her over very well and said she is gaining weight and appears to be in good health. He gave me some vitamins for

Eunice and said to bring her back in a week. Today she is a beautiful lady with two children and two adorable grandchildren.

Chapter Fourteen

We had a nice house and car when we got in the Far East. Our new home was in a good area of the city where government officials and members of various embassies lived. We had a four bedroom home with a nice court yard and walls around our home. The walls were seven feet high made with stone and concrete with pieces of glass embedded on top. Because of the large Military presents and my Department of Defense ID card, we could use the Commissary and Exchange. Both are similar to the Walmart stores we have here in the States. We could also go to the Officers Club and Theater. I thought it was a very good assignment. At first our new life was alright with my wife. She had a hard time making friends and that bothered her. Maybe it was because of her heavy smoking, I don't know. And after a few years of not knowing where I was or when I would be back she started to turn against my work. She didn't know what I really did. A few years later I told her, but I shouldn't have. I will explain more on that later.

Our rough-tuff son Clint was over two years old and had a dog that he loved and the dog loved him. They played hard together all day and slept together at night. Eunice was a beautiful little baby girl. When she was less than one year old, our Maid started to take her around to her friends in the baby buggy. Our Maid had lots of friends in the city and loved to show Eunice off because she was so small, light skinned, and had blond hair. As she got older her hair got longer and curly so she was the talk of the city. She would be sound asleep when she got home and would sleep the rest of the day. Clint was hard on his toys. Every day the Maid would take the broken ones, sell them and with that money plus fifteen cents, she would have an arm full of new toys.

We all enjoyed the people and the food. After we were in the States a couple months, my son asked if we could find the same kind of food here that we had overseas. There was a carry out restaurant near our home so once a month he and I would go there, get the food he liked and bring it home for the family to eat. Most of the time he and I ate it with chop sticks.

My work at that station was routine except for two projects. One was during the War when my partner, a local agent and I were sent behind enemy lines to photograph documents at a headquarters building and destroy a radio station. We trained, worked hard and practiced every move and with alternatives. This project had to go perfect or we would all be killed. We parachuted in and all went as planned until we were on our way out. We were on a narrow road in the semi-dark of the day when I heard some talk. I jumped to the right and my partners jumped to the left. We tried to hide but there was very little to hide behind. As five enemy soldiers started to pass us they spotted my partner and our local agent. They pointed their guns at them and said something which I didn't understand. I was behind the soldiers so I jumped up and pointed my pistol at the one with strips. Our local agent told them to lay their weapons on the ground or I would shoot. They did and as I turned to ask my partner what we should do with them, I heard a string of tap, tap, tap. I turned around to find that our local agent shot them all with his machine pistol with a silencer. I said, "Gees", why did you do that. He said did you want to take them home with you or did you want them to take you to their home. I said OK, let's get them off the road and get out of here. That is war, the same as at the radio station and the headquarters building. I didn't like it but war is not a play game. It's kill and destroy or be killed and I knew that before I accepted the project.

One of the things we parachuted or jumped with was a little three man folding boat that we hid. We retrieved it, took it to the bay and tried to get in it. At home we practiced until we could get in it with only one person getting his feet wet. In our hurry here, we tipped it over three times and we all got soaking wet. We paddled as fast and hard as we could, not only to get to the submarine but to get warm. After an hour of paddling, tired, wet, hungry and thirsty, I gave one short signal flash and kept on paddling. Every half hour I would do it again. After some time my partner whisper, what will we see first the sub or the states. After a couple hours more the sub started to surface one hundred feet in front of us. What a pleasure and relief to see it! Life on the farm was not like this. I wish my brothers Bill and Leo could be with me now. They would have enjoyed this project. The three of us would have been a real team.

One evening I had to attend a party at an Embassy. As I arrived the Host asked me what kind of drink I wanted. I said I'd like a soft drink. He said "NO"; I'll have a good drink made for you. He thought I was there as a guest but I was there to work and do what I was trained to do. A few minutes later I was handed the drink. I tasted it and it was terrible but I told him it was good. I had to play the game. When I met someone I knew I asked him what it was and he told me it was scotch and water. I said I don't like it. He said you have to acquire a taste for it. Every time I saw a potted plant I gave it a little drink if no one was watching. I then remembered back to my days in the Bakery. I wanted to be like the big boys and drink coffee. We kids on the farm never drank coffee and I didn't like it. When I told the guys I worked with that I didn't like it, they said I would have to acquire a taste for it. I did, and always wished I hadn't because now I love it. But; I will never acquire a taste for Scotch Whiskey and water.

Another project that didn't go as planned was getting a Doctor from another country that we were not friendly with. I don't know what kind of Doctor he was or what his specialty was. Everybody in CIA has a top secret clearance and that clearance allows you to know what you are doing, what your job or project is and nothing else. If you are captured you can't tell the enemy what you don't know.

My partner, a different local agent and I had to go across the straits, about fifty miles of water. We had a boat built to look like an old fishing boat with a one cylinder diesel engine. But everything under the water was a high speed boat powered by a large mercury engine. When we arrived our local agent went ashore to get the Doctor. When he returned he had the Doctor and his wife. That was bad. My orders were to bring the Doctor back, but he would not go without his wife. I had no place for her on the boat and everybody on shore could see her getting on a fishing boat, plus women did not go fishing with nice clothes on. I just knew that someone would call the authorities. I told everybody that if and when I holler, ON THE FLOOR, I want you all to lay flat and spread out. I started the diesel and got out of the harbor when I saw the gun boat coming around the corner about half a mile to a mile away. We had guns but no match for a gun boat. I said, on the floor, we're going to run. I jettisoned the little diesel engine, started the big engine and pushed the throttle full forward. The boat lifted up and we were flying. They started to shoot and we were hit twice with what I thought were 30 caliber rounds. It was dark with no moon and after five or six minutes I thought we lost them. Then we got hit with a big round. It went in near the top of the boat and came out near the water line. That had to be a lucky shot. How could they see us?

We were going about seventy miles per hour. I wanted to turn my body around and look to see where they were and how my passengers were especially the Doctor because without him our project would be a complete failure. At the speed we were going the boat was very unstable and when the shot hit, I almost lost control of the boat. So I had to keep my full attention on the boat. I was standing, steering the boat and felt something hit my leg. All this time the boat was just skimming on top of the water. I slowed to three quarter throttle and made a slight turn. After about five minutes I turned on the compass light for a second and got back on course.

My project officer was at the dock waiting for us. I turned the Doctor and his wife over to him and then noticed my leg. I found that I had a piece of the boat in my upper thigh and a boot full of blood. A local Doctor cleaned it and stitched it up. While I was at the Doctor's office, my partner fixed the hole at the water line so the boat would not sink at the dock. The next morning we took the boat out to very deep water and sank it. Six months later I went to an American Military Doctor because my thigh etched and looked bad. He said it was OK. Six months later I went to another Doctor for the same reason and he too said it was OK. A year later I couldn't stand the etching and the scar looked terrible. I bought a bottle of whiskey, razor blade, tweezers and bandage. I put a lot of whiskey in me and some on my thigh. I cut and washed the blood off with whiskey. The whiskey hurt and burned so bad that I kept putting more inside. I'm starting to like the taste. I kept that procedure up until I felt something about three quarter of an inch down. A little more cutting and a little more whiskey and there I found a piece of the boat. I pulled it out, washed the wound with the rest of my good whiskey, put on the big bandage, and pulled it tight with tape. A short time later the etching stopped and in a few years the scar was gone. I should have been a doctor. "Doctor Don". I like the sound.

Another time we had a project that took place on top of a mountain. The people in that country were either very rich or very poor. The poor men had bodies and muscles like a horse. Before my partner and I went up the mountain we employed three local men to carry our equipment and help with our project. When we had them loaded with all of our equipment they asked, is this all? I didn't think they could carry it all and they thought it was a very small load. My partner and I were in very good physical condition but after a mile or two up the mountain we were worn out. Our locals took our back packs and after another hour we were behind so far that they wanted to carry us. There was no road and our path was just a rocky trail. They were so strong and in such good condition that when they walked with all of our equipment on their backs their muscles moved up and down like the muscles of a horse. They climbed that mountain as if they were mountain goats. Our work on the mountain was classified so I can't say any more about it.

On the mountain I don't know if it was the strenuous exercise and clean fresh air or if we just didn't bring enough food along but we ate our entire two week ration of food in one week. Our locals brought some food and the rest they got off the land so we joined them and ate what they cooked and ate. I didn't know most of the time what I was eating but I was staying alive and feeling great. We finished our project and started down the mountain. Going down was harder than going up even with very little to carry. Maybe it was because I had lost ten pounds. I don't believe our locals lost an ounce. They looked and acted as if the trip never happened.

Chapter Fifteen

We returned to the United States for a thirty day vacation in Minnesota with our families and then on to Washington, D.C. Our Parents really enjoyed being with and playing with their Grandchildren. They had grown a lot in three years and were healthy and very active. We rented a cabin near a lake near where our families lived and spent a lot of time on the lake fishing, riding in a boat and swimming. Clint really liked to fish and be in a boat on the water. When he caught a fish you could hear him completely across the lake. Eunice was a pretty little girl with long blond curly hair and just wanted to be hugged and played with by all the family. When our vacation was over none of us wanted to leave but it was time to go. I still have a job.

Chapter Sixteen

We drove to Washington, D.C. and I reported to my project officer. He told me that I would receive training in a different field but still as an undercover agent. The training was again fun and exciting. I also learned a new language, not well but good enough to get along and to do my job. I taught my son some of the words and he enjoyed talking to other kids in that country when we got there. After one year in Washington, DC we were assigned to a station in the Middle East. My wife Doris was pregnant and again, she would not go to the Doctor. I asked for a delay on going overseas but was turned down again since there was no letter from a Doctor. This time she was eight months pregnant.

We left on the assigned date. For three days we traveled, waited and changed planes three times. Finally we were at our new station. My office had a nice little apartment for us until we found a home. That night at one o'clock in the morning, Doris said, I think the baby is coming. I didn't know where to go or what to do. I went outside and started walking. A few minutes later I met a man. With my poor new language, he showed me where there was a two bed American Dispensary. There were less than one thousand Americans in that country so that government would not allow us to have a Hospital or Military type store. Our baby boy Travis was born in the morning and that evening Doris had to leave the Dispensary because they needed her bed. Doris did not breast feed any of our children and in that country anything good and safe to eat was hard to find. The Doctor told me about a place that might have baby formula but it would be expensive. Mother's in that country always breast feed their babies as long as they could. I found some formula and Travis survived on it. Now I have another problem. I have a foreign born son. At eighteen years old all boys in that country are automatically in the Army. At one week old I took a picture of him and applied for American Citizenship. Three weeks later I received it then I had to apply for an American Passport and visa. Two months later I received that. Now I have a son with dual citizenship. Then I had to apply for a resident permit so he could live at our address in that city. Travis has been in that country over three months without a resident permit and that is against the law. When I told the authorities my story, they wanted to put me and Travis in jail. I had to take a policeman to my home and get Travis. On the way back I stopped in my office and got an interpreter. After some fancy talking, dancing and arm waving, I showed them Travis' birth certificate for both countries, his passport and visa. Finally, they were convinced that he was only a baby in my arms. I had to pay a $ 50.00 fine for having Travis in that country illegally. After I paid the fine they said he could stay with us. (That was very nice of them.)

It took some time to get used to living in that country. Safe food was hard to find. Anything eaten raw had to be washed in Clorox water first. Everything else had to be cooked well done. Water had to be boiled before you could drink it. The electric was very low or off most of the day. We would cook our meals after eleven in the evening and warm them up the next day to eat them. We would take our shower at eleven or twelve at night then fill the bath tub with water to use the next day. The water that was not used that day, we would use to bathe our children in. After eleven in the evening the water pressure would be about fifteen pounds of pressure. Most places in the states the pressure is forty five to sixty five pounds.

I did all the baking, bread, cookies, cakes and Doris did most of the meals. I also learned to sew to repair a seam or let out our children's clothes because it was hard to find good clothes there.

My counterpart in that country was an Army Major. My job was to train him and five junior officers to do our kind of work. He and his junior officers were all hard men but easy to train. They were also men you did not want to cross. I believe fighting and killing was part of their life and in their blood.

One day he told me that he and I would go hunting for Wild Boar Saturday morning. He never asked me anything, he always told me except in our training. There I did the telling. Guns were not allowed in that country and I wondered what we would use to kill Boar. I said OK but we don't have guns and wild boar is dangerous. He said "I am a Major and I have guns." Saturday he picked me up with his jeep and he had two rifles, both old bolt action with a four shot clip. When I loaded mine it looked like it was not cleaned and oiled in a long time. He said when we see one there will be two or more with it. We will both shoot and if they charge at us we will jump up and let them go between our legs. It will take the boar a minute to stop and turn around then we shoot it again. The woods, shrubs and brush were very thick. It was hard to walk and I wondered how we could see any kind of animal. Then we saw two boars. We fired at the same time and one of us shot one in the head and killed it. As I was trying to reload my gun, it jammed. The major reloaded, shot, but missed. The boar turned and run back from where he came from. I asked him? What are we going to do with it because I knew they didn't eat pork in that country? He said we are going to eat it. That sounded good to me. Before we loaded it onto his jeep we had to do the normal hunter "YUCKY" thing. I didn't like the mess but it had to be done. We took it to our tent and he told his cook how to prepare it. For the next five days he, his officers and I had pork every day. We ate everything but the bones and the squeal. As we left, his officers said it was the best wild meat they ever ate and wondered where we got it. We didn't tell them.

On the way to another project by myself in a pickup truck loaded with classified equipment, I stopped for lunch half way to my destination. The owner of the restaurant was very nice and friendly with a good handshake. Although I didn't trust him and no one else, even an undercover agent has to eat and sleep. That nice friendly man poisoned me. Did he think I would pass out on the road and get killed? Half asleep and very sick I continued to drive to the next town. I stopped at the police station and passed out. They notified the American Embassy and a policeman guarded my truck until help came from my office. For five days everything that was put in me came out the top, bottom and my pores. For years after that everything I ate had to be cooked well done or soaked in Clorox water. That continued even after we got back in the States. In this kind of work you never know who your friends are. Everything is by chance and a gamble.

In all the countries I worked in, there was one thing they all had in common. When we had a meeting with high officials of the government or military, we would first have a cup of tea and talk about the weather and family or something other than business. When our cups were empty then we would talk business. Once as we finished our tea the senior officer told his servant soldier to come in and take the cups. As he entered, the young soldier was told to close his ears because we were talking about a classified matter. If the soldier would have said anything to his friends, he might have been beat to death or near death. That Army didn't have a jail or stockade. They didn't need one.

One country that was poor did not always have the kind of tea that we are familiar with, they would have whatever was in season from flower blossom to acorn or a grain. I can't say it was good, only different and something to remember.

When I had about six years with CIA I started to think that if something happened to me, no one would really know what I did and who I worked for. I wanted to tell one of my brothers that I trusted but that would take a letter and I didn't trust the mail. So I told my wife which I later discovered was a mistake. Every time she was unhappy with me she would threaten to tell on me. I told her that is a sure way to get me killed or captured. Then on my last tour of duty overseas, when I got poisoned, she said if I don't quite today she would tell on me to all her friends. I told my

Chief and he said a man is coming in to be assistant chief of security for the station. He said you take that job until your time is up, which was only six months, and the new man can do your field work. My wife was OK with that and we finished our tour.

We had a couple friends from that country that we visited and they visited us. We enjoyed their food and company and they ours. One couple wanted to come to the States to visit and maybe stay but we never heard from them after we left. Their food was different and it took a little while to get used to it. After we left none of us missed it. We were glad to have American and Japanese food.

Chapter Seventeen

As soon as we had arrived back in Washington, D.C., I put my Wife and the two oldest children in a hotel and I took Travis to the Hospital. I told the Doctor his history and told him that Travis never looked or felt good all his life. He is over two years old and just started to walk. After the Doctor examined him and made some tests, he said you are lucky that you brought him to me when you did because in one month he might have been dead. He gave me a big bottle of liquid medicine and some pills. He said be sure to bring him back in one week. I did and the Doctor said he was improving but it will take at least eight months for him to get good and healthy. Today he is a big strong healthy man with a family.

A little over seven years total in four different countries, my wife said that is enough. I was offered a job at the CIA Headquarters in Washington and would be assigned to the training department. There would be no traveling and I would be home every night, but my wife said no. She wanted me away from that kind of work all together. I was not only satisfied with my work but I loved it plus the pay was very good. I also loved my wife and children and would do anything to keep them happy, together and satisfied. So to have piece in the family I resigned.

Chapter Eighteen

I talked to a friend that had a friend in the Photography department of the White House. My studies and a lot of my work were in Photography. I called him and after a long talk he asked me to fill out some forms. I did and a few months later I got a job in the White House Photo Office and worked with Cecil Stoughton, President Kennedy's personal photographer.

When I started to work, Cecil told me to work in the photo lab for two days and get to know the lab personnel. The second afternoon at about two o'clock, Cecil called me and said to come to the White House right away. He had an emergency at home and in an hour President Kennedy would have a guest and I should take pictures. When I got there Cecil was gone. I was never in the White House before and of course not in the Oval Office. The Guard told me where the Photo Office was. Cecil had told me earlier that when the little red light comes on, I should go to the Oval Office and take the pictures. I asked and was told by a Secret Service Agent where the president's secretary Mrs. Lincoln's Office was. When I returned to the Photo Office the red light was on. I was so excited that the only thing I could think about was going to the bath room which I didn't have time for and knew it was only nerves. "I'm going to the office of the President of the United States" WOW. I am not prepared or trained for this! This is too much too fast! Mrs. Lincoln took me in the oval office. I took several pictures and turned to leave and to my surprise Mrs. Lincoln was gone. I saw three doors separated by only a few feet and didn't know which door I came through. After a few seconds that seemed like an hour I picked one and it was the right one. Had it been a rest room or kitchen, I might still be there. I was so nervous. This is really different from my CIA work. There we worked through and studied our project before we did it.

There was a lot to learn fast. I was told that I was doing a good job but I thought that was hopeful thinking. This is BIG with lots of important people. Can I really do it? Always looking my best and saying the right thing! The pressure, perfection and importance were stronger, different and greater than when I was in CIA. Plus in CIA I was trained in what I was doing. This is all very new and different than I am use to. What did I get myself into this time? I kept telling myself, I can do it. Never give up. Never quit. Nothing is too big.

My first trip with the President was to Amherst Massachusetts. I was excited and nervous the whole trip. This was big. Riding in the motorcade, in the vehicle behind the President, walking with him and taking pictures of everything he did that was important for historical, political or personal reasons. I took lots of pictures and could hardly wait until they came back from the lab. Cecil was satisfied with my work and that made me feel good.

When I was riding in the motorcade I sat between General Clifton, the Military Aide and Doctor Berkley, the Presidents Physician. I noticed that they were waving to the crowd. Then the General told me, when you ride you wave. The people standing alongside the route don't know who you are but they know you are some body important or you would not be in the motorcade. That is when I became a politician. After that I never passed up a chance to wave or shake hands. A few years later President Johnson told me that shaking hands is good for the heart, and sometime after that I read in a medical journal that hugs and handshakes have a huge beneficial effect not only on the heart but on the whole person. (If you work in the White House or running for public office, it's also good for votes.)

The next trip was to Dallas Texas. Cecil asked me to take it but at the last minute he said he would take it because he had a friend there he hasn't seen in years. That is where President Kennedy was killed. I was glad I wasn't on that trip because it required more experience than I had. Cecil knew everybody that worked close to the president and could move around easier that I could have.

I was in my White House Office which was near the Secret Service Office checking over some proof prints. An Agent barged in and said the President has been shot. I said NO, CAN'T BE. He said it's true. I asked in disbelief, how bad? He said, the first report doesn't sound good. I was too stunned to say anything else.

Who was behind the killing? We will not know for one hundred years after that terrible day. The Secret Service Agents always did the best job possible and you could always spot them because of their 38 caliber bulge. It was a pleasure to work with them but total protection is impossible.

I am often asked why the President was killed. There are lots of possible reasons. He was involved in the Cuban government problem, the Bay of Pigs invasion, the Russian missile problem, Integration, Civil Rights, the Mafia, the Berlin Wall in East Germany and the Viet Nam War. The polls showed that half of the Americans believed we would go to war with Russia, plus other big problems involving the United States. President Kennedy faced some unprecedented challenges.

I often thought some of his problems were caused by himself and his advisors such as the Cuban problem. Fidel Castro was a Guerrilla Fighter in the jungles and mountains of Cuban. He was backed by the United States government to overthrow the Dictator President of Cuba. When he succeeded, Mr. Castro became the President of Cuba. He then flew to Washington for aid to rebuild his county. He still looked and acted like a Guerrilla Fighter. He didn't play the game laid down by the White House. He didn't wear a suit and tie nor would he stay in the Blair House, the official resident for visiting dignitaries. He was rejected by the White House so he went to the Russian government. I believe that if President Kennedy and his advisors would have given him time to change from Guerilla Fighter to President and counseled him, all the trouble could have been avoided. Then there was the Viet Nam predicament. It had started as an internal Viet Nam Government complication. We should have stayed out of it. I also believe that because most of his advisors were family or close friends, there was very little difference of opinion on most subjects.

I knew John F. Kennedy and Lyndon B. Johnson did not get along. Johnson wanted to be the President not the Vice President but the Democratic Party wanted Kennedy and

Kennedy needed the state of Texas to win and the only way was to get LBJ to run as Vice President. Now only a few years later and after a terrible misfortune, he is the President.

Was President Johnson involved in the killing of President Kennedy? No one will ever know and I don't want to guess. I will say that while I was counting, forty six people died that were investigated because of the assassination. President Johnson appointed a special commission to investigate all aspects of the assassination. It was comprised of highly respected leading officials from the government and non-government both Democrat and Republicans. The President wanted the country to move forward and put those outrageous claims of conspiracy behind us.

President Kennedy's first big campaign in office was a Medicare bill. It was completed by President Johnson and signed into law on July 30, 1965 in Independence Missouri at President Truman's Library. Bills are signed using several pens and President Truman was given the first pen used on the Medicare Bill. The reason President Kennedy was very interested in Medicare was due to the fact that his own bad health started at age two. Over the years he had all the medical diseases and problems that children have then adult diseases and then a very bad back dilemma. Most of his life he was in a lot of pain but he didn't let the pain stop him from going forward. In the 1960's most of the time he was taking as many as twenty six pills per day mostly for pain. During WW II he wanted to join the Army and was turned down. Then he tried to join the Navy and again turned down but through his Father he did get in the Navy and served as officer in charge of a PT boat. Although the President had a bad back and constant pain, I often thought that he was more interested in sports, family, friends and especially girlfriends than in his office. He enjoyed playing all kinds of ball games, sailing and power boating. Every afternoon he would swim in the White House Pool for exercise. After work in the evenings he sometimes enjoyed watching WW II or western movies. President Kennedy and President Johnson both often worked late in the evenings at their desk in the Oval Office.

Mrs. Kennedy didn't like to be First Lady. She would rather have been a good wife and mother which she was. Jackie tried hard to create a perfect environment to raise their children. She was often seen on the south lawn playing with her children. When we went anyplace people wanted to see the President and the First Lady but Jackie always took the spot light. She had that dazzling smile that won the hearts of everyone. Everybody also wanted to see their two young children but Jackie tried hard to keep them away from the public so they could have a private life and be a family.

President Kennedy was known as the classic charismatic leader and had a higher approval rating the first year than any other president in modern history. It never fell below seventy two percent. Now, years later the public faithfully ranks him atop the presidential charts but, historians voted him the most overrated public figure in American history.

I met President Johnson when he came back to Washington after the assassination and that is when the long days started. We had to photograph the funeral of President Kennedy and everything about the new President. Those were very long days. I missed meals and sleep. It reminded me of my CIA days when we were on a project, and also when I was going to high school in Morehead Minnesota. It's hard to think, anticipate and foresee when you're hungry and tired.

When the funeral was over and President Johnson was settled in the White House, Cecil wanted to ask the President if he could go on a trip to Paris with Mrs. Kennedy. I told Cecil not to ask because President Johnson didn't like the Kennedy's and he would fire him just for asking. He said he was going to ask anyway. He did ask and was fired. He then went to Paris with Mrs. Kennedy. I don't know who paid for his trip but when he returned he got another job in the Washington DC area.

There was a big difference in working with President Kennedy and President Johnson. President Kennedy was friendlier and family oriented. President Johnson was, in a way, unfriendly, a hard man to know and the hardest working man I have ever known. He was well-known for his face-to-face confrontations and putting his finger on your chest. If there was a small reason he would verbally assault you using some unkind words. He always wanted everybody around him to work, to stay busy. At the Ranch one day he saw a communication man standing next to the communications building doing nothing. He told him to get the lawn mower and cut the grass. He got a lawn mower, cut the grass then went back to work in the communications building. Once I heard him tell a White House Staffer to clean out your desk, you don't work here anymore. That was in front of a lot of people. Very embarrassing and I have never known him to apologize. I listened, watched, learned and got along well with him. He could see that I was working hard and trying to keep up with him.

About two weeks after he fired Cecil I got a partner and we tried to take turns going on trips.

Now I am the President's personal photographer, projectionist and armed courier and sometime protection. I was with him and his family on most trips and every day in the White House. What an honor and pleasure it was standing or setting next to the most important person of the free world.

President Johnson was a big man, six feet four inches tall, weighed two hundred and forty pounds and was always full of energy. When he walked into a room his energy filled it to bursting. He was a tidal wave. He had the ability to work with congress and world leaders and he knew how to make a decision. When he had to make a big decision he would call a few of his advisors and consultants and tell them to get all the information they could on the subject, pro and con and be back in two days to report their findings. Two days later they would return and all would go into a small room off of the Oval Office. When the meeting was over the President would go to his desk. Using the knowledge he had plus what he just received, he would make his decision and never look back wondering if his decision was the right one.

He got a lot of Bills through congress and always had a Bill Signing Ceremony in the Rose Garden. He was never without an idea, and was always planning and working on something that would improve the United States and the World. In his early days as President he said there are three things he must work on, Peace, Prosperity and Medicare. He was very passionate about health care issues and education for all Americans. Health care was important to him because of his own brush with death when he had his heart attack. And he understood education because before he got into politics he was a school teacher. He also wanted to cut the Welfare Program. He said there are too many people drawing government assistances. Unfortunately the press was against him on that program and it didn't get very far. Another thing he wanted was to balance the budget. He asked all government heads to cut wherever they could and to set an example he was going to turn off all the lights in the White House at night, which he did. One evening I was asked to do courier service and was told to come to a room in the basement at eight pm, and be sure to bring a flashlight because it is really dark going down those steps. Another way he wanted to save money was for all White House employees to travel by commercial airline whenever possible. Mrs. Johnson decided that she too should fly commercial when possible. Several times I flew on a commercial plane with her. She would wear a hat, an ordinary dress; carry a hand bag and a book. She looked just like any other lady her age. Their two Daughters did the same except they often wore a wig and dark glasses. Mrs. Johnson and her Daughters were very beautiful and ordinary ladies; they could fit in with a crowd when it was necessary and not be noticed.

The President was a very smart man that talked a lot. If you listened you learned. He seemed to be his own FBI & CIA man. Every morning he spent time speed reading the newspapers. The hardest time for him was when they would tell him how many men got killed in Viet Nam on that day or week. I saw him put his head down and I don't know if he prayed or cried, maybe both. I think that war killed him a little every day because like the Korean War, it was an unwinnable war. He tried everything he and his advisers could think of to win that war and it hurt him that he couldn't. I don't think he ever lost anything in his life that he got involved in. He was always a winner except in this war. Every day he would see the demonstrators on TV around the

White House. He could also see them from his living quarters. He understood what they wanted, but could he give up, quit and run? Not the winner LBJ, but he knew he couldn't win it and every day it came closer to killing him.

He was the hardest working man I have ever known. If you worked with him you had to at least try to keep up with him. He often called a staff member back to the office after nine or ten o'clock at night. Three times I was called back to take pictures. I was with him on his second trip to the Johnson Ranch in Texas after he became President. At 10:30 pm I was in my motel room getting ready to take a shower and go to bed when I got a call saying the President wants you. I quickly dressed again, got into my car and drove to the Ranch. I knew the President didn't like to wait so I drove as fast as the car would go. At 100 MPH I hit a striped pussy cat. I was afraid to drive into the yard because I thought of the smell. I stopped a long way from the house, got out of the car and there was no smell. I guess I was going too fast for it to spray. When I got in the house the President asked me what took me so long. I said I was in town in my motel room. He said I want you to move into the Guest House tomorrow morning. After that I stayed with the Military Aid, the President's Doctor and the President's Assistant now called chief of staff.

He had his gall bladder surgery in the Navy Hospital in Bethesda Maryland. He woke up at three o'clock in the morning and wanted to know where his staff was. After that, many of us stayed in the hospital until he was discharged.

On one trip to the Ranch Mrs. Johnson asked me to come with her to the President's Birth Place. She had some friends with her to see where the President was born and she wanted some pictures. After I took some pictures for her, the President called and asked me to come to where he was showing one of his Prime Bulls. I looked to where he was and thought, if I drove my car it would take twenty five minutes to get there but if I walked from the birth place I could be there in ten minutes if I run and crawled across or through a fence. I decided to run and cross the fence. With my camera and camera bag I run and tore my trousers crossing the fence. When I got there the President was standing to the rear of a bull with his friends. He said take a picture of this and he lifted up the bull's tail and said to his friends, isn't that the best looking bull you ever saw. The only place he ever relaxed was at the

Ranch and even there it was mostly business. I learned early on the job not to forget to say, yes sir or no sir Mr. President. Only his very close friends could call him Lyndon, all others must say sir and Mr. President. His language was not always nice and his stories were no better. One evening he had a small party in his living quarters and invited a few of his friends from the Senate. The language the President used in telling stories would form a very dark cloud, something a lady or gentleman would not want to hear.

On another trip to the Ranch, one of the telephone operators told me that I must see a Beer Bar in town because it was very unusual. I told him if the President knew I was in a Bar, he would fire me. But he kept telling me about it on every trip we were on together. So one afternoon I went with him. I told him I would just look and leave. When we walked into the Bar, the Bartender came walking over to us with a quart jar of beer and said the first one is on the house. I tried to say no but he put it in my hand. I carried it around as I looked and saw that the bar had a dirt floor and the bar stools were saddles. All the wood in the bar and the building was rough and unfinished. There was a four piece band playing "Waltz across Texas". Now when I hear that song I can see that Bar in my mind. It was all very unusual but I had to get back. Everybody in the bar walked me out to my car and wanted to talk about my job with the President. I told them if I didn't get out of there and get back to the Ranch I wouldn't have a job. Those few minutes were very enjoyable and without a drink. I will always remember that place and the nice friendly people that were there.

Most Sunday's the President and Mrs. Johnson would go to church. One Sunday the President, Mrs. Johnson, some of his cabinet members and a few congressmen went to a catholic church. They took up two pews. The President asked me to take some pictures of them. I went in, took some pictures during the service and I was sure the priest would say something about interrupting the service but he didn't.

The President and Mrs. Johnson were always good to me. When I would show them movies in the evening, the President would sit next to me and give me popcorn from his bowl and made sure I had a soft drink. If we were outside and it was hot Mrs. Johnson would tell me to take a break and have something to drink.

One time when Mrs. Johnson had a large party on the south lawn of the White House, I was working with her and she said: Don, take a break and have something to eat and drink. I went to a tent where there was food and drink and the first thing I saw was a chocolate éclair. I love chocolate éclairs. I picked one up, took a bite and everything inside came out of the bottom and run down the front of my cameras. Then I heard Mrs. Johnson say, "Don", would you come over here a minute please? I looked at my cameras and the lens was covered with the stuff from inside of the chocolate éclair. I walked slowly while I wiped my camera lens first with my necktie, then my suit coat, then my handkerchief. It was still a mess but it worked.

All the times that I spent Christmas at the ranch, after the party was over the

President would ask me to sit down at his desk. He would ask me about my family and give me a gift for them, usually a box of candy, and then he would give me a special gift in addition to the nice large White House Christmas Card. Once it was a beautiful small pocket knife with the presidential seal on it. Another time he gave me an invitation for my wife and me to attend a state dinner and dance, and always something for my children.

When I showed them movies in the evening I had to stop at ten o'clock. The President would watch the news on his TV and Mrs. Johnson would watch Gun Smoke on her TV in another room. The Presidents first choice for a movie was a documentary involving him and his next choice was anything Mrs. Johnson and their guests liked. Most times if the President's Daughters were along I would show then movies in the Guess House after I finished in the main house with the President & Mrs. Johnson and their guests. Sometimes they would have a guy friend that was recommended and introduced by the Military Aide or the Presidents Aide. I would finish showing the girls their movies at around 230 am, put everything away and try to get a few hours of sleep. Most days when we traveled or was at the Ranch I would eat a fast breakfast and a very late dinner. If I tried to eat in the day time, as I sat down or half way through my meal the President would call me for something. I paid for numerous meals that I didn't eat before I got smart and stopped trying to eat in the daytime. Everyone that worked close with the President was expected to work long hard hours. At times I felt like I was working thirty hours a day and eight days a week.

Being with the President and the first family was a true and a great honor, something money could not buy. Working with President Kennedy, President Johnson and meeting President Truman and President Eisenhower was a great honor plus some members of the House, Senate, all of the members of the President's Cabinet and some Governors. I met and got to be friends with Vice President Herbert Humphry. Many of the pictures I took during my years in the White House were of State Dinner Parties, Bill Signing, Fundraises and get together with family and friends. They were for Political, Historical and Personal reasons. Most may be found in the LBJ Library in Austin Texas.

It was very hard on my family, not being home most Christmas's, Easter's and many other important family days. One time when I came home my Son said, Mom there is a stranger in our house.

I didn't want to but it was time to leave The White House and the President. BUT, now I felt trapped. How do you quit the President of the United States? I didn't tell the President I was going to quit, I asked him if I could and told him why. He accepted my reason. It took six months to find a replacement for me. My last trip with the President was at his Ranch and He and The Frist Lady wished me luck in my new job.

Before I left the White House I was asked by a staff member to do one more job as a courier. When I was with the CIA and the White House, one of my jobs was that of an armed courier, always with my ivory handle 38 special. In all those years I have delivered briefcase's, boxes, money in a money belt and other things that I carried in my hand or belt.

    I told the staff member I would and he told me to be in room 28 in a down town building at five o'clock the next morning. Rush hour traffic doesn't start until about six thirty so at that time of the day there was lots of room to park. I parked at the front entrance of the building. I entered the building and walked down the long hallway. The last door on the right was room 28, next to the exit door. I went in and the only person there gave me a round trip airline ticket to New York City, then he handcuffed a large briefcase to my wrist. I was given the pass word and counter signs. He said there is a white sedan parked at the exit door and the drivers name is Ralph. Outside of the exit door a man said, I'm Ralph, you want the front seat or back. I said front but after I got in

I found I didn't fit with the big briefcase handcuffed to my wrist and my seat belt on so I changed to the back seat.

This was very scary because I knew if someone wanted it bad enough they wouldn't try to pick the lock on the cuffs, they would separate my wrist from the rest of my body. I didn't know what was in the briefcase and didn't ask because it was none of my business. My job was to deliver it. Ralph took me to the airport and let me out at the ticket counter. It was normal for the pilot to sit me in the front seat of first class because I carried a gun. I was on my way to New York. When I got off the plane my hand was either on or very close to my 38 special. In a crowd I heard the password and saw the yellow button. I followed him to the men's room a few feet away and gave him the counter sign and he gave me the right sign back and said walk ten feet behind me. At his car he said get in the back and he would drive. I had my hand on my 38 and got in. In the back seat was another man. He introduced himself and stuck out his hand. I knew that trick so I stuck out my 38. He said you won't need that and showed me the hand cuff key with a yellow button. He unlocked the cuffs and handed them and the key to me. We drove around the airport and I was let out at the ticket counter. When I arrived at the Washington airport the same car and driver was waiting. I got in, went to the same place I started and handed the same person the cuffs and the key. I wiped the sweat from my forehead and went home.

After five and a half years I left the White House. For a long time I missed working with the President. I missed the song

"Hail to the Chief", the handshakes, and everything that goes with working next to the President, the most important person of the free world. I still think about it but I'm glad I quit when I did because the hours were just too long and I was away from my family to much.

Chapter Nineteen

Most people around the world have seen the outside of the White House on TV, in newspapers or magazines but very few have seen the inside. The Oval Office is a very business-like office and highly respected. The only people I ever saw in the Oval Office without a coat and tie were members of the Press when they were invited in. The desk of President Johnson sat at the front of his office, with a chair on one side. The President sat with their back to a bullet proof window. The carpet was light blue with the Presidential Seal on it in front of the President's desk. In the center of the room there were three chairs and a davenport or settee plus chairs along the side of the room. He also had a teletype machine and three TV's. One for each wire service so he could see and hear what the newscasters were saying about him and world affairs. On the walls were beautiful scenery pictures and pictures of long past distinctive people. The Oval Office and rooms in the Presidents living quarters are changed or redecorated with each administration. In the Cabinet Room, which looks out on the Rose Garden, there was a long table with straight back chairs all around it and some chairs along the wall. On one wall over the fire place, is a painting of "The Signing of the Declaration of Independence" and is flanked by marble busts of George Washington and Benjamin Franklin. In the main house, the Blue Room was painted blue and the furniture is upholstered in blue. The doors and window frames were painted white and the lower three feet all around the room was a white paneling. The Red Room and the rest of the rooms were decorated like wise. In the State Dining Room is where all the State Dinners were held and from there all the Guests would go to the East Room to dance and socialize. It is the largest and most formal of the state reception rooms, and most of the time the only piece of furniture is the Steinway grand piano. The Lincoln Bedroom is decorated with American Victorian furnishing. His bed is more than eight feet long and nearly six feet wide. President Lincoln first used that room as an Office and Cabinet Room. Some years later the East Wing and West Wing were added to the White House and the President's office and Cabinet room were moved to the West Wing. Then President Lincoln's office and Cabinet room became part of the family living quarters. Years later, President Truman renovated the White House and converted that room into Lincoln's bedroom. Outside on the southeast side, Jacqueline Kennedy had a Rose Garden planted. It was always very beautiful. There were always lots of beautiful flowers outside around the White House that were changed with the season.

Chapter Twenty

Now that I am unemployed I called CIA and asked for a desk job in Washington. They told me that they had a one year job for me without my family overseas then I could be in Washington until I retired. The overseas job sounded interesting. I talked to my wife about it. She didn't like it but I told her that with the money we made and saved so far, we paid off our home and two cars plus put some aside for our three children's college education. I told her I didn't want our children to get a college loan and spend the rest of their lives paying it off. One more year of hard work and we would be set for the rest of our lives and we would never be separated again. When I get back I'll have an eight hour a day job and wherever we go and whatever we do, we will do as a family. And the first thing we will do together is go to

Niagara Falls. A place we talked about visiting for more than a year. I needed a job and this job really sounded like it would be the kind of work that I would enjoy, plus it paid well.

After a two week refresher course I left for an assignment in the South East Asia area. I was to work with the local police chiefs along the border of that country. It was never necessary for me to cross the border. They worked with the army and knew about troop movements across the borders. This information cost me a bottle of whiskey and a case of beer once a month for the chiefs that I worked with. The year was routine except for the repair of a large Radio Transmitter station. It was in my district so I was asked to repair it because it had stopped working. They knew from my record that I had a year of electronics in high school and when the industry changed from the vacuum tube to transistor I took one semester in college. In high school I made a radio transmitter and did a lot of electronic repair.

I drove to the city near the radio station. The Chief of Police there knew about the transmitter and told me it was about six miles from town and less than four miles of that was on a hard road. I asked him if I could leave my vehicle at the Police Station. He said yes, it would be a good idea because it would not be safe to leave it unattended on that road. That was a long walk with 110 degree temperature. At the end of the road there was a narrow trail, all jungle. I cut a stick about five feet long and as I walked I moved the stick back and forth to clear the way of snakes and spiders. I was alone with my 38 special as my only companion. At one place on the path or trail I saw what looked like a very large harmless Bull Snake. He hissed at me in his aggressive way so I hissed right back at him. Neither one of us got scared away so using my five foot stick I gently moved him out of my path and kept walking. I heard animal sounds but kept going and tried not to be afraid. About fifty feet from the station a monkey jumped on me, knocked me down and before I could get my 38 out he had taken my cap and was gone. I told the station operator about it and he said that monkey is his friend. Every time he comes to the station he brings some food for it and talks to it.

At the radio station I asked him for his test equipment and all he had was a small electric meter. Then I asked him for the schematic for the radio. He said he never saw one. I found a very small one with the radio installation book. After an hour I found the problem and asked him for the parts kit. He said that he didn't have one. This is always normal in a foreign country. I don't know if they lose it or sell it. Sometime later I found the part number for the complete circuit board. It was too late to go home so I stayed there and ate the food I brought.

I left the next morning and told the station keeper I would be back in a few days. He said be sure to bring food for the monkey.

As I approached the station on my return trip, I held a banana out in front of me. About fifty feet from the station the monkey appeared, flying out of the jungle and dropped down in front of me. He looked at me with his monkey smile and took the banana and run. "I yelled", WHERE IS MY CAP, but he kept going.

Chapter Twenty One

My year is up and I'm told that my position would be eliminated. I enjoyed my work, the people and the food. I made a recipe of some of the special food dishes that I liked and made them when I returned to the States. My son Clint especially liked the one called "Cawpot". I never gave it an American name. It is made with rice, carrot, onion, peas, meat and egg then all fried together. It will be good to get back to the states, home, and to my wife and children whom I missed and love very much. What a joyful time we will have, never be apart again. My wife and children wrote to me often but that will never replace touching and being with them.

Chapter Twenty Two

My plane landed in San Francisco California at six in the morning. My brother Leo lived and worked in the area so I called him. It was good to hear his voice again. He told me that our Mother had died yesterday and would be buried in our home town in Minnesota. I asked him when he was going to Minnesota. He said he wasn't. He wanted to remember our Mother as she was when she was in good health. It was hard for me to understand but I knew my brother and for him, it was normal to say that. I told him I wanted to see her once more and also see our family and friends.

I called my wife in Virginia and asked her what time she and our children would get to Minnesota. She said they would not be there but gave no excuse.

I went to the ticket counter and got a ticket to St Paul where my brother Frank lived and another ticket for Virginia. The plane would leave in one hour. I called my brother in St Paul and he said he would pick me up. I called my wife and asked her to pick me up at the Washington airport at eight thirty in the evening two days later. She said; take a taxi home because I have a date. I said this is no time for jokes or kidding around. She said I'm not kidding, I mean what I said. I could not believe what I was hearing. I sat down on a chair trying to comprehend what she just said. Was that my wife?

I started to look around and I saw young people without shoes, holes in their clothes, long dirty hair, and a blanket around them.

They looked just plan dirty and worthless. I can't believe any of this!! Am I dreaming? Is all this real? My Brother, my Wife, these people? What about my children? Is this what I spent a year in a combat zone for? Something is wrong here. I was trained to see and hear everything but do I really want to see and hear this???

I looked at my watch and it was twelve noon. WHAT?? Where am I? I missed my plane! Did my brain go into shut down mode due to extreme stress and shock? A Psychiatrist or Psychologist would have a fancy name for it but all I know is that I was out, lost in a corridor of my brain. I'm sure that I wasn't sleeping because I had just slept twelve hours on the plane.

I got a new ticket. I called my brother in St Paul, told him I missed my plane. He said he just got home but would go back and get me when I arrived.

He did pick me up and we drove one hundred and eighty miles to the town where our Mother would be buried. There were a lot of people there that I haven't seen in years and some since my catholic school days. They were all so very proud of me and what I had accomplished since I left home. I don't remember much because my mind was on my children and what my wife said.

Two days later my plane landed in Virginia and I took a taxi home. Our son age 12, daughter age 10 and son age 7 were all on the floor playing. They didn't know what to do or say because they knew what their Mother had been doing. For 14 years she was a good wife and mother. She always put my needs and those of our children first, she always kept the house clean and cooked good meals, but now this!! I don't understand!! I guess I worked too hard to make a good living, a good name and a good future for all of us. She came home late that night and the next day she packed a suit case and said she was going on R & R. (Rest & Relaxation) A man pulled up in his car to get my wife. Didn't she tell him what I did? That I worked for the CIA as an undercover agent and that I work out every morning, that I was very strong, that I had training in karate and could kill with one blow!! As I stood next to that car and wondered, what could she be thinking? Very reluctantly and with great restraint I held myself back, struggling with myself and thinking the whole problem through before I acted as I was trained. I knew if I got started with those two they would both go to the hospital and God forbid, maybe die. I would go to jail, maybe for a long time or life and then who would take care of my children. I turned and went back into the house to take care of my children. OH, my poor children. They are too young for this. I wanted to cry, I wanted to destroy something, but could not in front of my children. I must be strong. Never give up, never quit. Have positive thoughts. I can get through this.

She left with the guy.

Two weeks later she returned and said she wanted me out of the house and that she wanted a divorce. I asked why? She said the guys will buy her all the cigarettes and beer she wants and she doesn't have to answer to me. That sounded like beer joint lawyer talk to me. I asked her to wait until the children were older. They are now at a very tender age and a divorce could hurt them the rest of their lives. I told her that I loved her and we can make our marriage work if she would stop this foolishness. She would not hear any of it. She just wanted me out of the house. I don't know why I still loved her, maybe because she was the mother of our beautiful children. I cried and felt very sorry for our children. I know now what they have gone through in the past year and the worst is yet to come for them. Because our home was in a big turmoil and everything so confusing we didn't go to Niagara Falls or any place else. It was time for me to become "Re-Americanized" like so many military men had to do over the years when they returned to the States from a war zone. The war is over for me. I will never go overseas again. I have my Children and a long life in front of me. I will not give up.

When I was young I compared my life to a road trip from New York to California. If the road was under construction I wouldn't stop there until it was repaired, I would make a detour and keep going. Now it's time to make another detour in my life. Keep thinking positive and very soon life will be back to a new normal.

To have a full life you must always have a plan and a goal. If you don't have a goal and a plan to reach it, you will never know where the end is. Never stop, never slow down, keep going full speed ahead. I promised myself that I would make it, but I felt so sorry for my children. What a terrible time they will go through and I can't stop it. I asked my wife to go with me and talk to our Church Minister but she would not go. I asked her to go with me and talk to a Medical Doctor friend of mine. She wouldn't go. Our children told me they had not gone to church since I left. For years we attended the local Methodist Church as a family and our Children enjoyed the Sunday school classes very much.

My home life was unbearable and outrageous. It was very humiliating the way my wife treated me and what she said in front of our children. She just wanted me out of the house, so I moved out with just my clothes thinking that I could come back later and get the rest of my things.

Is this what I worked long hard hours for, making extra money for our children's education and our retirement, an honest respectable living with a good name, living in constant danger as an undercover CIA agent? It would be easy to feel defeated and hateful but I am too strong for that. I have no hate or animosity in my heart for anyone. I forgive and move on. Hate and stress can contribute to or cause heart attacks and strokes and I'll have no part of it.

I then transferred all of our money into my new bank account. I can no longer trust her. I knew what it cost to support the family so every month I gave my wife that amount of money.

During the next two weeks I had several job offers. I decided to leave CIA and find a job in another field as long as it had to do with photography. I was offered and accepted a job at NIH at the National Cancer Institute doing micro and macro photography and electron microscopy. It wouldn't be open for two months and I knew I needed more biology so I started school again and then night school when I started work. I really liked the work. Eight hour work day with nice people. It was very rewarding because I always felt I was working on that dreaded cancer disease that I or some loved one might contract. Three years after I started work I received credit in an American Medical Journal for my work in Cancer Research.

A few months later I designed and built a Test Tube Photo Copier. After I made a few changes on it I gave it to the government. It was reproduced and used by other medical photography departments.

Two years after our separation we got a divorce and the judge gave everything in the house to my wife because he said I abandoned it. I lost all the white house pictures that I kept and all the souvenirs from around the world, some were very beautiful and expensive. I was told that Doris my now ex-wife, later sold some of the very expensive items for very little money just to feed her habit of drinking and smoking.

The judge said I had to pay her alimony for two years, beautician school for two years and child support until our children are of age. Also I had to pay all the court costs and legal fees from our savings. When I took the alimony and child support out of my pay check plus my living expenses I had forty dollars per month left. Many times before we had children I asked her to get a job but she never did. During the next few years after our divorce she had several jobs but none lasted long. I was told that she stays out late at night and sometimes doesn't come home or comes home too drunk to work.

After our divorce my ex-wife would take me to court every month or two. Once she went three months without taking me to court and I thought she had stopped doing that. But she didn't. The judge would always dismiss the case but I had to pay both lawyers and court cost. Once the judge told her to stop using the courts time and just be thankful that her children had such a good father. He visits them every week and always paid his child support on time. She didn't hear any of it because the court cases continued. After some years the court and legal fees were eating me up. The Judge always ordered me to pay both lawyers and court cost. My savings and the money I saved for our children's college education was running short so I quit school and got a photography job. I worked in the evenings and weekends.

Chapter Twenty Three

I enjoyed doing weddings, parties and portraits, especially weddings although everybody told me that my portraits were beautiful. In photography school I received a special mention award for a portrait that I did earlier of a General that worked in the Pentagon. Every Saturday I had a wedding to do. The next day I would go to that church if the Priest or Preacher was nice. One elderly Priest in a Catholic church was not nice. He stopped in the middle of the ceremony and said to the bridesmaid, why don't you get married and make babies and later when I was taking the wedding party pictures, he told me I was doing a very bad job and all I wanted was their money. I didn't go back to that church. Another one I didn't go back to was a Methodist church. I always took a picture from the far back of the church during the wedding without flash or sound. This picture showed everything from the ceiling to the floor and all the people. After the wedding the Preacher really got after me for that. He wouldn't let me take pictures of the wedding ceremony during the service. Then he got quite upset and unhappy because I asked him to do the re-enactment of the wedding ceremony so I would have pictures of the wedding for the newlyweds. At the wedding reception his wife verbally attacked me even more extreme for that one picture. What a nasty, cold, cruel woman she was. A very bad example for a Minister and a Ministers wife. I don't know where she was during the wedding because I always took that picture just inside the rear door. What she said really hurt me and the pictures I took at the reception showed it. Most Priests and Preachers were very nice, one especially. He was about five feet five inches tall and about one hundred and seventy pounds. His name was Harvey Edge, Pastor of the Church of God in Rockville Maryland. When I asked him how he would like me to do the wedding pictures, he said any way you want. He and his wife were very nice people and it was a beautiful wedding. The pictures I took at the wedding and the reception were some of the best I ever took because the pastor and everybody were so friendly and kind. The next day I attended his church. In his preaching he said that to go to Heaven you must be saved. I went to Church every Sunday when I could most of my life but I never heard that before and according to the Catholic Church I was going to hell. He showed me in the Bible, Romans 5:8 where it said: But God commended his love toward us, in that, while we were yet sinners Christ died for us. In

Romans 10:9 That if thou shalt confess with thy mouth the Lord Jesus, and shall believe in thine heart that God hath raised him from the dead, thou shalt be saved. In Romans 10:10 For with the heart man believeth unto righteousness; and with the mouth confession is made unto salvation. And in Romans 10:13 For whosoever shall call upon the name of the Lord shall be saved. I told him that I wanted to be saved. He then asked me to pray and ask Jesus to forgive my sins because He was the only one that suffered and died for my sins. I said, should I say a Hail Mary or what? He said "Nooo" that is not praying, that is reciting a memorized verse that you learned. The dictionary definition of pray or prayer is: to talk, ask, offer praise, petition, entreaty, beseech, communion with God. He said when you pray, just talk to God the way you talk to me, and in Jesus name. I then asked Jesus to forgive all my sins and come into my heart and take control of my life, 1 John 1:9. Later I was baptized the Bible way, by emersion because that is the way Jesus was baptized in Mat 3:16. Every day since then I read from the Bible and Pray. Life still has hills and valleys, ups and downs, good and bad but now I know that the spirit of God lives in me and helps me in all that I do and say. I like to think that God gave me a heart transplant because now I see everything differently. My biggest wish is: I wish I would have been saved years ago. I feel that all my life I played with religion. I was an altar boy, sang in the choir, and told the Priest my sins, everything a good Catholic does. I believed there is a God and Jesus Christ, but I never accepted Jesus as my Savior and really didn't know him as I do now. Now I have a real relationship with Him. I talk to Him off and on all day and he speaks to my new heart.

Knowing Jesus is like knowing a neighbor. You really don't know your neighbor or Jesus until you have a close friendly relationship with him or her. That might be hard to understand until you get saved.

Chapter Twenty Four

One Sunday afternoon as I was driving around I noticed a nice and very attractive pink and white house on the corner of a street. It had a For Sale sign in front and also an Open House sign. The outside of the house and yard looked clean. Having nothing to do, I stopped and looked at it. The inside was a disaster. I could see light through the roof. The kitchen, bathroom, living room and bedrooms looked like pig pens. As I was walking out the Salesman ask if I was interested. I don't know why but I asked, how much? He said $24000.00. I told him that would be a normal price if the house were in perfect condition. He said make an offer. I said $10,000.00. He laughed and said, give me a $500.00 check to hold. I gave him a check and told him don't cash it because it's no good. All my money is tied up in divorce court. What am I saying? I don't want this decrepit building. The neighborhood is nice but this house is rubbish, plus I have no money. Some body will buy it because the Lot alone is worth $10,000.00.

Ten months later I received a phone call. The voice said congratulation, you just bought a house. I said you got the wrong number and hung up. The phone rang again. It was the same guy. This time he said you just bought the pink and white house on the corner. He said bring $1000.00 more and we will have the $1500.00 down payment. The rest we can finance. Settlement will be in one month. Very fast I had to borrow $500.00 to cover the check I gave him and in one month I needed $1000.00 more. I had some, the rest I borrowed from a lot of friends. I had the money that I had set aside for my children's education but I didn't want to use that. I thought if I started using that, I might not stop. But it didn't take long and I had to use it to pay the lawyers and court costs, all for nothing because the judge always threw my ex-wife's case out.

I bought the house, moved in but didn't have enough money to buy a broom. I borrowed cleaning things from a friend that I worked with and got the house presentable. It was a three bedroom house so I advertised for two roomers. The first week I got a nice Egyptian man that worked nearby. His name was Mick. He agreed to help me put on a new roof and fix the house up so I gave him a good price on the rent. The next week I got a lady that worked at NIH as a medical artist. She was very good at her job and made a good income. She had a teenage daughter and they agreed to cook, keep the house clean and share the master bedroom. I gave her and her daughter a good rental price. The Mother's name was Kitty and her Daughter's name was MaryAnn. The four of us became good friends, shared the price of food and worked on the house every chance we had. In two years we had a new roof and the inside was completely re-done. I built a work shop in the back yard and repaired the driveway. I had borrowed money from Mick and Kitty so now I had to make payments to them, the friends that I borrowed money from to buy the house plus I had a big house payment. That left me with not a cent for myself. I have not failed yet in anything I started and I will not fail here.

My children met Kitty, her daughter and Mick and thought they were all very nice. A little later when I would go and pick up my children, Kitty would ask if she could go along. Her daughter had her friends from school and Mick had his from his place of work. Kitty and I both worked at NIH so we drove together to and from work. It appeared that we were always together. About two years after we met, Kitty suggested that we get married. She said that she loved me and never wanted to be away from me. I thought about that for a week and although I didn't love her, I thought in time I might. We have been together for two years in the same house but not the same bed. I could see nothing about her that I didn't like, so I said yes. A month later we got married with my children, her daughter, her two sons and friends from both of our places of work in attendance. The only change at home was that I moved into the master bedroom with Kitty and her daughter moved into my room.

We left on our honeymoon and planned on being gone a week. The first day of our honeymoon she changed. What did I get myself into? I thought it was because she missed her daughter so we stopped our trip, turned around and went home. For the rest of our married life she was the same. I don't know how she could be a phony for two years. I think she had all this well planned. Everything I said or did was wrong. Her family and friends always came first. She liked to embarrass me whenever she could and the more people that saw or heard it, the more she laughed and the better she liked it. Do I have to put up with this? Is this the way married couples live? First Doris turns on me after being married for fourteen years and now Kitty turns on me after only one day. What can I say? It's too late, we are married and I don't want another divorce especially so soon.

Thinking it through, she did keep her word about cleaning the house, cooking and helping to fix it up. So; I'll try to put up with her fashion, the new women I just met after a one day trip. Maybe I'll get use to her and maybe, even love her someday.

Eight years after I bought my little pink and white house, we sold it for $ 60,000.00 and bought another house to work on. Now it was only Kitty and I.

I asked the court to let my children live with us because the two boys were always in trouble. The police would take them home and their Mother was never there. The Judge said no, they belonged with their Mother. In those days a Mother could not be bad enough to lose her children. Clint wanted to live with me and later did without the courts approval. Eunice said she had to stay there and take care of her

Mother. Travis said he didn't want to leave his friends. I wanted to put both boys in a Military School but the judge said no. So everything stayed the same.

Chapter Twenty Five

After eleven years I was out of money because of the lawyers and court cost. I had no savings or money left for our children's college education. It appeared to me that Doris my ex-wife wanted to destroy my life and that of our children. I asked my lawyer how long this can go on. He told me, it can go on until you are dead or move far away.

That night I talked to my wife Kitty about it. She suggested that we quit our jobs, sell the house, everything we own, buy a travel trailer and go to California. That is what I wanted to do also but I wanted to hear it from her. The only problem with that was: I would be cheating my children out of having a Dad close by. That really bothered me but I had to do something. If I didn't pay the lawyers and court cost I would go to jail. With my work at the Cancer Institute and my Photography job I had very little time for myself, my wife or my children. Most of the money I made was going to the lawyers and court costs. I did not get paid for the time off from work plus each time I went to court I had the cost of my travel expenses from Maryland to Virginia. Kitty was now paying a large part of our living expenses which I really appreciated.

Chapter Twenty Six

We sold everything and bought an Airstream travel trailer and a Dodge pick-up truck. We went to California, Arizona and Texas but didn't care for any of them. Then we went to Florida and settled in Key West.

On our way to California we stopped in a small farm town and noticed that they were giving away baby chicks. We got one and bought some chick food. Then I got a small box, electric cord and small light bulb for heat so the chick would stay warm. All he would do is peep unless I held him, so I held him a lot. As he grew older I found that it was a Rooster so I named him George. I trained him to go potty on the paper and later to go outside. When he would hear a bird, he would try to imitate the same sound that bird made but it never came out right. He didn't know he was a chicken. He would follow me around like a little puppy dog, he never wanted to be alone.

After we were in Key West for a while and George was a year old, a friend from Kentucky that I served with in the Army back in the 40's came to visit us. He was retired and had a little gentlemen's farm, a cow and calf, a horse and twenty five chickens. I told him that when he leaves to take our chicken old George with him I don't want him any longer. He was getting to be a real pest, he never wanted to be alone and I guess I didn't have time for him anymore. Anyway, my friend took our rooster and two weeks later I got a letter from him. It said as soon as he got home, the rooster wanted to get in the house and he had a hard time keeping it out. Then it took over the outside area around the house. When his dog got close to the house the rooster would chase him to the barn and if a chicken got close to the house he would chase it to the chicken house. When he put chicken food in the trough for the chickens, old George the rooster, would chase all the chickens away until he was finished eating plus he was always fighting with his chickens and some stopped laying eggs. So last Sunday they brought him in the house and had him for dinner.

Poor George, he finally got to do what he was born to do and that was to grace some ones dinner table.

Chapter Twenty Seven

After a couple days in Key West Florida I got a job as Dive Master on a dive boat but first I had to be a certified master diver. I was a certified basic and open water diver so I took the master diver course, passed the test and worked every morning as a dive master on a dive boat. I really liked that job. I could dive every day and get paid for it.

Sometime later I had an accident with one of my divers. I always discouraged my divers from using a spear gun. There is so much to see in the ocean and on the ocean floor that a spear gun is not necessary. Most would not listen to that. They wanted to shoot a fish and there was no law against it. In all that time no one ever shot a fish. One day a young lady with a small spear gun shot me in the back. I went to the surface as fast as dive law allows. Blood will draw sharks and we didn't want sharks in the area, especially one that wanted some of my blood. She was about ten maybe fifteen feet from me with that little gun so the tip only went in me about one half inch or less. She cried all the while other divers were in the water and all the way back to the dock. I thought she would suffer from dehydration. I felt so sorry for her. I put a bandage on it and the next day kept working as Dive Master. In a couple months it was healed and there was no damage done. It was a good educational story for the divers on the rest of my dive trips, and no more accidents.

One day on a dive trip alone, I was diving in about fifty feet of water and saw a very large grouper fish. I wanted him but being in a hurry I didn't get a dead shot. He went into a cave with a small opening. I looked in and there he was next to a sleeping nurse shark. Because the opening was too small for me and my dive gear, I took off my air tank, laid it and my regulator aside, reloaded my gun with another spear, and went in the cave, shot the grouper, backed out pulling him with me. I then put the regulator back in my mouth, started breathing again, strapped the tank back to my back, took my thirty nine pound groper to the surface, got in my boat and went home. I sold it to a Restaurant for $5.00 a pound after I cut one steak for myself and Kitty.

Another exciting and almost fatal day is when another diver and I went diving with a full tank of air. We both shot a few fish and got two lobsters each. We dove until our air tanks were empty then got back in the boat. After sitting in the boat about a half hour I decided to snorkel awhile. I was in the water about ten minute when a five foot hammerhead shark appeared. Each time he came close I would use my spear gun to push him away. It's stupid to shoot a shark with a spear gun because instead of killing him you will only make him mad. After pushing him away about five times, like a flash he bit my spear gun and pulled it out of my hand. About twenty feet away he dropped it. As he swam away I looked and saw my spear gun was on the ocean floor. I didn't know how deep it was, I just wanted my spear gun. I started down and discovered that it was deeper than I thought. I kept going and all at once I saw very pretty lights and heard very beautiful music. I knew that was a sign that I my body and brain had run out of air/oxygen and only had seconds to live. A few more kicks and I had my spear gun. I went to the surface as fast as I could and lay on my back on the surface for a few minutes. My dive partner helped me into boat and we went home with me on my back. When we got home my wife asked my partner what happened. He told her and she said; he has cheated death so many times that she has lost count. I had a bad headache for two days but I had my spear gun, with only a few bite marks.

Most of the time I lived in Key West Florida I never wore a shirt or trousers, just little shorts. My skin was a very dark tan from the sun, almost black. With my back ground at the Cancer Institute I don't know why I never thought or cared about getting cancer. Just living a very carefree life having too much fun I guess. Now for the pass twenty years I have some skin cancer removed every year.

A very wealthy man from Michigan told me that he had a house on the island and wanted someone to open it and get it ready when he, his family and some friends come down about once a month. The pay he offered was very good so I said yes. A month later he told me he wanted to buy a 55 foot cabin cruiser and needed a Captain. I told him I would get a captains license and work for him. I took the course, passed the test and got my license. I went with him to buy his boat and it was a beauty with twin diesel engines very nice inside and a pleasure to operate. Every day he was on the Island we would go out fishing, diving or just for a ride. I'm having fun and getting paid for it. I can't believe it.

Then I got to know a man that was seventy years old and had a very nice Motor Cycle. It was a Honda, 750 super sport with all the extras. I asked him one day why he never rides it. He said once he was run off the road and into the ditch. That scared him half to death. Another time a driver went through a stop sign and missed him by an inch. And once he went to the store and as he was putting the kick stand down, the bike fell over on him, hurt his leg and arm. He said that time it was his own stupid fault but it hurt bad and took a long time to heal. He said if you want to buy it I'll sell it to you cheap. I asked how much and he told me. I looked it up in the blue book and it was half of the book price and it had less than one thousand miles on it. I bought it and when I wanted to register it I was told that I needed to complete a driver training course. It was a two day course. One day in the class room and a one day driving class on an old parking lot. It was offered by a policeman that was a licensed instructor. After the course I knew that no one should ever get on a motor cycle without completing that course. One very important thing I learned and experienced was that car drivers see in their minds-eye, cars and trucks but not motor cycles. I came very close to having an accident because they didn't see me, although I always wore a bright yellow jacket and a bright blue helmet.

I rode it whenever I had time and several times Kitty and I took a long trip. One fall of the year we went to the Mountains of North Carolina, The scenery was really beautiful, spectacular. And one summer we rode to Minnesota and then on across the Continental Divide in Colorado. It was beautiful but scary when I drove near the edge of the road and looked down. We saw a lot and rested a lot because you can't ride very far without getting very tired, sore and hypnotized. We enjoyed our trips and always looked forward to the next one.

Then I met an elderly couple in church that was 93 and 95 years old. They needed help in maintaining their home, going to the doctor, shopping and going to Church. I did as much as I could for them and after I got to know him he told me that he was a Bee Keeper in Ohio before he retired and moved to the Florida Keys. That sounded very interesting and the more he talked the more I wanted bees for a hobby. He had six hives but only one was still alive. He said I could have his hives and all the equipment he had. I took it all home and started buying all the books I could find on bee keeping. I found out that bees have been around for a long time and are first mentioned in Genesis, the first book in the Bible. With only one hive I didn't know if it was good or almost dead. So I bought a Queen Bee from a honey bee company in Ohio. They sent it to me in a little box through the US Mail. The Post

Office delivered my Queen as soon as they got it because they didn't want a Bee in the Post Office. With the Queen were four worker bees in the little box to take care of her. Queens cannot take care of themselves. I then started another hive.

The more I learned the more I loved my bees. One of the many very fascinating things I learned was that in a hive with 50,000 bees, not one bee is in charge. God gave each bee the ability to think on her own and if she lives a full life time, she will bring to the hive one teaspoon of honey. All worker bees are female. Male bees do nothing but mate with a new queen once in her life before she starts laying eggs. That fall I had more honey than I could use so I gave some away to my friends. When I run out, my friends said, now you got me hooked on honey and you run out. So I started another hive. Every year it was the same. When I sold my honey bee business I had over one hundred hives and still not enough honey. The last year I had my bees I took off and sold four thousand pounds of honey and could have sold more. I sold honey in stores, restaurants, flea markets and from my home. In the winter some people from up north would come to the Florida Keys on vacation and buy one or two gallons and a few bought a five gallon pail of honey so they could share it with their family and friends when they got home.

One year after I started I designed a label for my honey containers, and then I had to get registered with the State of Florida. That required me to pick up swarms that landed on cars, buildings, boats or trees. The first time I got a swarm I got stung about twenty times so I designed and built a honey bee swarm collector. After a couple changes, I could pick up a swarm in fifteen minutes and not get stung once. Stings didn't bother me. I read and was told by old bee keepers that stings are good for arthritis. I believe that to be true because of all the beekeepers I have known, none had arthritis.

I continued working on the dive boat, took care of my friend's house and worked as a boat captain and now I'm a bee keeper. Once a month I would write an article for the local newspaper about bees. Every week in the winter I would give a lecture about bees at a school or a civic group. I lectured once at the Florida State Bee Keepers Association. I taught bee keeping to four men in the lower keys and sold them enough bees to get them started. When I gave a lecture I was always invited to come back because there was so much to talk about. I also grafted my own Queen Bees because it cost too much to buy them. A Queen is good for only three or four years and a young queen is better than a good old queen. Grafting Queens is a very delicate and tedious skill. Bee Keepers from north of Florida wanted to buy Queens from me because I could start them much sooner than they could. I had to say no, I just didn't have the time.

I must stop saying this but it's true. I can't believe I'm having so much fun here in Key West and getting paid for it. We have a very good church here that I help in and God blesses me continuously. We give ten percent of our income to the Church and five percent to the Hope Children's Home in Tampa Florida. Hope Children's Home is supported totally by donations from individuals, churches, business and organizations. They receive no government funding. They are licensed to have eighty children and their Director is a Baptist Preacher. Since 1968 they have cared for over 5000 abandoned, abused, neglected and orphaned children. Years later when Irene and I were visiting the Director, a man and woman drove up in a nice car, he got out, picked up a small suitcase, took a four year old girl by the hand and walked her into the Directors office and said here is another one for you and he left. A week later the little girl came to the Directors office and asked? When is my Daddy coming back? He never did come back. Visiting that home and the children in person will leave a scar on your heart. They are truly God's little angels. For twenty five years Irene and I have been praying for and sending support to cover two children in the home. www.hopechildren'shome.org

I continued to send child support to the court for my children by way of a third party. My Son Clint is in the Army and my daughter Eunice has a job so I only pay one third now and in a few years my youngest son Travis will get a job. Twelve years after our divorce Doris my ex-wife died from liquor and cigarettes.

Chapter Twenty Eight

A lady friend of ours showed me a ski cap she got some place overseas. She asked me if I could make a needle so she could make some caps for her grandchildren. I started working on it, trying to make a needle from wood. It didn't work because I couldn't keep the grain or fibers from catching the yarn. I tried a Plexiglas Rod and after several weeks I had one that would work. The problem was in order to get the kind of Plexiglas rod I needed, I had to buy a big box of rods eight feet long. I talked to my wife and her lady friends and they all said I could sell lots of them if I tried. I then built a machine to make the needles and over the next ten years I sold thousands of them to make ski caps, afghans and shoulder warmers. I also printed instructions on how to make those items. I called it a "cro-knit needle" because first you put the yarn on the needle crocheting and then you would turn the needle around and knit taking it off the needle. I had two sizes, one twelve inches long for baby afghan, ski caps and shoulder warmer and one twenty four inches long for a full size afghan. If you used two different colors of yarn, when you were finished you had one color on one side and the other color on the opposite side. I sold the needles and my honey at all the flea markets and hobbies & crafts shows that I could find. I also sold needles to hobby and craft stores wherever I traveled and by mail order.

Chapter Twenty Nine

My wife Kitty was keeping busy with art work, sign painting and hobbies. Sometimes she would go with me on the dive boat and snorkel over the divers. She also enjoyed fishing but could not when divers were in the water.

After ten years of marriage she started going to visit her children, brothers and sister more often. She would usually be gone for two weeks. She said I shouldn't go along because none of them like me anymore. I didn't know why because we always got along. I thought they were nice people, but I didn't ask any questions.

One time she was gone for over a month and when she returned she said she wanted a divorce. She wanted to marry her high school sweetheart. I asked why, I thought you loved me. She said I never loved you. I liked you but I didn't love you. I married you so I wouldn't have to be alone. What a blow that was because I always considered her a good wife. Not the best but after I got used to her ways and her lying we got along.

We divided all our property and a week later we were divorced. When her boyfriend asked his wife for a divorce she beat the tar out of him and they stayed together. Then, my now ex-wife wanted me to marry her again. I said absolutely not. She told me more lies in the years that we were married than I could count. The big one before we got married was that she and her first husband still owned a farm in Maryland. About a year later she said her ex-husband sold their farm, forged her signature and kept all the money.

I didn't want to give up any of my jobs. I enjoyed being a dive master and a boat captain but most of all I loved my bees. I never met a bee keeper that didn't love his bees. It's all they want to talk about. Maybe it's because all the worker bees are girls and every beekeeper I met liked girls especially their wife. My wife put a sign over the door saying: don't ask my husband about his bees.

I lived on the Island six months more to sell my honey, cro-knit needles and my bee business. Then it was time to move on and away because my ex-wife wanted our house and wanted to continue living there. She lived alone and died six years later of colon cancer. When I heard that I remembered telling her at least once a year to go to the Doctor for a checkup. She always got mad at me and never went once in all those years.

I went to Minnesota to visit my Brother Bill. He had several lots on a lake so I stayed there all summer in my Airstream travel trailer. I knew Bill and his family spent most of their summers at the lake. One summer when I went there he had a chain and lock across the road. I couldn't turn around with the Truck and Airstream travel trailer so I picked the lock. When he arrived and saw the chain was unlocked he really got mad until he saw me. Then he asked me how I got the lock open. I told him I picked it. He said I thought you were a trained undercover Intelligence Agent working for the CIA. Now I'm beginning to think you are a trained crook. After a little drink, we talked about the times when we were young and picked the simple locks we had. It didn't take long and he was over his mad plus, I don't think he was really mad just teasing me. Visiting Bill and his family was always a pleasure and something I always looked forward to. We had a lot to talk about and stories to tell his children. It was one of those places that I never wanted my visits to end.

When it got cold I went to South Miami Florida. I like to square dance so I went to a square dance club hoping to find a dance partner. I met a single lady there that was also looking for a square dance partner. She was a good dancer so I asked her if she would be my partner next week. She said that she was a school teacher and if I would come to her house at six o'clock, correct her student's papers while she make her lesson plans for the next day, we could square dance from seven thirty to ten. That worked out very well and we danced twice a week.

She was a nice lady and we got along well. I met her two grown children and grandchildren that winter. The next summer I went with my Airstream Travel Trailer to stay with my brother in Minnesota again. I didn't write or call the lady I square danced with in South Miami but I was hoping she would still be single and dance with me when I returned. In the winter I went back to South Miami. The lady was still single and said she would love to square dance with me again under the same circumstances.

In the spring she took me to her Mother's house for dinner. After dinner she told her Mother that we were going to get married. Her Mother jumped up and gave me a big hug and a kiss on the cheek. My heart took a leap and missed a few beats. That subject never came up with us. Why did she say such a dumb thing? I said nothing. The rest of the evening I played the gentleman but when we got to her home I told her this is the end. I will leave tomorrow morning and have no plans to come back. She didn't want me to leave and I didn't want to but she pulled a dirty trick on me. I'm sure this will hurt her Mother but we are finished. I told her soon after we met that I had been married and divorced twice and would never marry again. I never ate at her house and never stayed over. She was unseemly not for me as a wife. I liked her for a friend and a good square dance partner but did not love her and did not want to marry her or anyone else. Two failures were enough. After I left I thought about our relationship. I wished she would have told me her thoughts before she told her Mother. I guess it's easy for a Lady to jump to conclusions when she thinks a man is playing with her heart, which I was not. I really feel bad for her Mother. But what can I do.

I pulled my Airstream down the road about three hundred miles and stayed in a campground. For the next two days I studied my Bible and prayed.

It would be nice to have a wife again but I told God, this time it's up to Him to find a wife for me. I know that since I have been saved, everything that he gives me is always the best. My problem is that I sometimes forget to ask him.

I traveled to Minnesota to visit my brother again for a few days and then on to the International Airstream Rally in Boise Idaho. Every day I would study my Bible and pray. I continued to ask God for a wife. At the Rally I asked two ladies at a singles table if they could square dance because every night they have square dancing at the Rally. They said no, they didn't square dance so I walked on. The next day one of the ladies that was at the singles table was at another table promoting an Airstream Rally in her home town in Wyoming. She asked me if I was coming to her Rally. I said no and walked on. I saw her once more at the rally but would have nothing to do with her because she looked like a country girl and I was a city boy. This was the third time I saw her in three days and there was over five thousand people there. God wouldn't put us together, would he?

A week later I started for Washington, DC to visit my children. At three in the afternoon it was time to stop for the day. I looked in my Campground Directory and found a campground in Douglas Wyoming. As I pulled off the interstate highway I saw a lot of Airstreams at the Fair Grounds. Instead of going to a campground I went to the Fair

Grounds. I wasn't sure but I thought it might be the Rally "that woman" talked about.

I attended the rally. It was five days long and very good. On the last day "that woman" came up to me and asked? Did you enjoy our Rally? I said yes and I was looking for you. She knew it was a lie because she said she stood next to me several times waiting for me to say something. The truth is that I forgot what she looked like and still wanted nothing to do with her, that woman, that country girl. I told her that I really enjoyed the Rally and it was one of the best Rallies I ever attended. That part was true. She said all this cowboy, horses and shooting was all put on for you city folks. I finally introduce myself. I said I am Don Stoderl. She said I am Irene Wallis and you're not going to change me. She was so nervous that she didn't realize what she had said until it had come out. We talked a little and I tried to get her relaxed. Then she said this is the last day of the rally and that she had a real live working Ranch. She said if I wanted to see how it is on a real ranch to be ready tomorrow morning and she would take me there. That sounded very exciting and interesting. I could not say no.

The next morning I was ready and I followed her to her Ranch. I really enjoyed my day at her ranch. Her two Sons tried to scare me off so I wouldn't get involved with their Mother. They didn't know it was impossible to scare me. The more dangerous something is the better I like it. At the end of the day I thanked them all and said it was time for me to go. She said no, you haven't seen it all yet, so I stayed another day and then left. Both days were very enjoyable. I wanted to stay longer but it was time to move on and not be a burden because I knew they had work to do.

On my way to Washington I could not get her out of my mind but I kept on asking God for a wife. After two weeks I was back to Key West Florida. The next morning when I was studying my Bible and praying, I had the very strong feeling that God was telling me, I found you a wife and you went off and left her. Was God injecting her into my life?

I wrote her a letter and she answer. Another letter and a few phone calls and we agreed to meet in Mesa Arizona where she had a winter home. We got to know each other and she learned to square dance. Five months later I told her that I would like to marry her but I don't eat like she does. I knew she was a rancher and ate red meat three times a day and that she was five feet two inch and a little fluffy. I told her that I eat about two or three ounces of red meat a week, weigh one hundred and fifty pound, feel great all the time and love my fruits and vegetables. I then told her if she wanted to lose her excess weight and feel better, I would do the cooking and she could work with me. She said she would, and did, and she went down to one hundred and thirty pound and felt like a new person. We were married in Mesa Arizona six months after we met.

Irene got saved in the Baptist Church in her home town of Douglas Wyoming a month later. The next month she got baptized in the same Church. All of that happened twenty nine years ago and we have never had words or raised our voice at each other. She is a true gift from God. When God puts two people together

He really knows what he is doing. When man does it, it can easily fail and often does.

Irene could now square dance and for a couple years we traveled around the United States sightseeing, square dancing and getting to know each other better.

I want to say something about the misconception of square dancing. I have been square dancing for forty years all over the United States. I have never detected liquor on a dancer and have never seen anyone smoke in the dance hall. Neither have I seen any sexual connotations in the hall. I have only seen respectable people with nice clothes, especially women with their colorful dresses. From the beginning, I have been told that square dancing is friendship put to music. It is very good exercise for the body and brain. After you take and complete the lessons, you can dance anyplace in the world because square dance calls are always in English.

We spent a few summers at her Wyoming Ranch which was a very enjoyable experience for me. We went horseback riding several times and I enjoyed it but I discovered that I would never be a cowboy. My butt is better suited for a padded chair. Then one day Irene's Granddaughter Tracy, asked me to help her bring in some cows and steers. I don't know why but I said I would. She got two horses saddled and ready. I wanted to say no, I have changed my mind but it did sound exciting and something I never done before.

We got on our horses and she started them running. I said no, can't we just let the horses walk? She said no, if we did that we would never get the job done. As the horses started to run I held on to the saddle horn with one hand. When we got to the cattle my horse knew what to do, he was well trained. We rounded up a big bunch and Tracy said this is not all. Then she said, you take these in and I'll look for some more. The cattle were bunched and in a line. After a while I saw one old cow fall back a little but thought nothing of it. I knew she would catch up later but my trained horse thought differently. It turned sharp right and started running. <u>I was not ready!!</u> I fell off the saddle and was hanging onto something on the left side of the horse. All I could see was cactus and sage brush flying past my head. I knew that this was the end of me. Then my horse was behind the cow and turned sharp left. I came up and on my way to the right side; I grabbed the saddle horn with both hands and held on. I looked up and saw the cow was on line with the others. When I got home Irene was waiting for me. She asked? How did it go?

I told her that I was going to take a shower, put on my coat and tie, sit in the recliner chair with a glass of ice tea and tomorrow I'm moving to town. I'm a city boy and city boys don't belong on a ranch with wild women and wild horses.

One summer a sheep had a lamb late in the season and its Mother just walked away and left it. When I found it I took it home and bottle fed it. It didn't take long and it thought I was its mother. I named it Bucky because it was a male. Wherever I went it would follow me. In the morning when I would do my two mile walk little Bucky wanted to walk with me. At first he would run and after a few minutes he would get tired and cry for me so I would walk back, pick him up and carry him the rest of my walk. When he got older he would stay home with the other pets, a dog, a cat, and a horse. He always wanted to get in the truck and go to town with us and sometimes he did but stayed in the truck and looked out of the window like dogs do.

The next summer my step son Bobby brought home a baby antelope that was about two days old. It was caught in a fence and its mother couldn't get it out so she left it. It had a broken leg and cuts all over. I doctored it the best I could and fed it lambs milk from a bottle. It grew, got strong and played with the other pets. We named him Smoky. Now we have a dog, a cat, a lamb, a horse and an antelope. If someone left the house door open they would all come in and Irene would give them all a kiss and then escort them outside where they belonged. They loved my wife and the kiss. In the fall of the year Bucky went to market with the other sheep that were born that year. Poor Bucky, I missed him. Smoky joined other antelopes but would come back occasionally and survey the surroundings. His horns got big so we never got close to him and he didn't want us to, he just wanted to be wild.

Chapter Thirty

We spent one winter in Arizona and since then we have been spending our winters in Florida. Square dancing is good and the beaches are beautiful. Frist we settled in the Florida Keys. We bought a nice home and a power boat. Most days we would fish, snorkeled and dive.

The ground was like concrete so I made a frame with concrete blocks and filled it with sea weed. It was the best garden and the most beautiful flowers that I ever saw.

The square dancing was good and we had a good church with lots of new friends. There was something to do all the time and it was all a new life for Irene.

Three years later we went sailing with some friends. I have always liked and enjoyed sailing and now Irene likes it too. We started looking for a big strong sail boat, one that we could live on and sail out in the ocean. Two years later we found one but it required a lot of work before we could sail it. Plus I wanted to take a sailing course and refresh my memory on navigation, weather, radio and all the rest. Irene also took the course and did well. A year later we sold our home, car, power boat and everything we had and moved onto our Sail Boat. I was used to living in an Airstream travel trailer but living on a Sailboat was new and very different for both of us.

Our new home was thirty seven feet long and twelve feet wide. It was big enough to be comfortable to live on and small enough for the two of us to sail alone. It had two very large sails and an inboard diesel engine.

We had everything in it that you have in your home, stove, microwave oven, refrigerator, sink with hot and cold running water and a dish washer also called First Mate. (Irene)

Our stove used alcohol to burn. It was slow but safer than gas. I baked bread and cookies in the oven. Irene fried and cooked things on top. Each time before we could use our stove, we had to use a bicycle pump to pump air in the alcohol tank to get the alcohol to the burners. For electric we had a diesel generator that used about one pint of diesel fuel per day.

Our first trip was to the Dry Tortugas / Fort Jefferson. It is about sixty miles from Key West Florida and a very interesting place to visit with endless history. It started as a very large military fortress. When it became obsolete they turned it into the nation's leading maximum security prison, holding several of the accused conspirators in the Lincoln assassination including Dr. Mudd. It is accessible only by boat or seaplane. We had a good trip going but that night we had a storm that lasted overnight plus four hours the next morning. The wind blew and the waves were about fifteen feet high. I wasn't sure if we could or even wanted to sail anymore. It was our first storm and it was not fun but we learned a lot. I was glad that I had the knowledge I gained as a Captain.

We found that when there was a problem or when anchoring, Irene was best at the helm and I would take care of the sails and everything else.

A few years later we met a couple that had a lot of money and an idea. They bought a fifty two foot sailboat with everything on it, a very beautiful boat. Their problem was: the boat was too big for them and they had no sailing knowledge or experience. They talked a lot but didn't listen. They forgot that God gave them one mouth and two ears so they could listen twice as much as they talked. One month out to sea and their boat was destroyed on a reef. They were lucky to survive and live through it. All their money didn't help them and their idea and planning was very bad.

The next trip was better and more fun for us. We had year round storms. The worse one lasted twenty four hours and had one hundred and ten mph winds and blew our wind gauge away. The waves were about twenty five feet high. I would always say that five percent of our sailing was very bad and dangerous but that left ninety five percent of pure pleasure.

We would set sail from our home port in Key West Florida after the hurricane season ended in October and we would return to the US when the hurricane season starts in July. On every trip out we always wanted to sail further so we would be out of the hurricane zone. Then we could keep on sailing for another year or more. But there was always too much to see and do. We didn't want to miss anything so we never got out of the hurricane zone. It's always best to see and do all you can the first time through. On our next trip we found an Island out in the ocean that was about five feet high, twenty five feet wide and two hundred feet long with a long reef on both sides. On one side of the Island it was ten thousand feet deep and beyond the Island and reef it was sixty feet deep. The name of the Island is South Riding Rock. To get through the cut in the reef you had to be sure you were reading the nautical chart correctly or you could get caught and destroy your boat. In situations like this, Irene would lean over the front of the boat and tell me with hand signals, right, left or stop. The water was always very clear. On the sixty foot deep side of the island there was a bed of Conch that was fifty years old or older because the shells were one inch thick or more. On our future trips we would set sail from the United States at one in the afternoon and arrive at the conch bed at sun up. I would dive all morning for the conch and in the afternoon we would clean them to eat and the next morning we would set sail. We would have conch meat enough for a month or two in our freezer When our conch meat was gone we would look for another bed. We brought some of the shells back to the states to give to our family and friends. From there we sailed to Chub Cay where we had to clear Customs and

Immigrations before we could sail any farther. Our Visa was good for one year. It cost $100.00 and included fishing and diving permits. Our next stop was New Providence Cay. One of the cities on that Island is Nassau which is also the capital of the Bahamas. It is a busy Port so we had to radio the Harbor Master for permission to enter. We stayed there several days. Walked around the island and ate lots of their good food. It's like any big city, everything you might want.

Before we left the United States we would buy enough canned and boxed food to last us for the months we were out to sea. I also grew alfalfa sprouts for our sandwiches instead of lettuce.

When we emptied a can I would cut the bottom out, smash the can and throw it overboard. In thirty days the sea water would eliminate it. We would keep our paper and plastic until we got to an island where no one lived. When the tide went out we made a little fire pit and burned our paper and plastic. Then when the tide came in it would take the ashes out.

It was really a different life and after a few weeks at sea we both loved it. Did Irene being a Wyoming Rancher, really enjoy sailing out in the ocean? Impossible!! I teased her and said the most water she saw before she met me was in a horse trough and now all she sees is water day and night for months at a time. She loved it and when we anchored and the boat was secured, most of the time she would be the first one to jump in the ocean for a swim.

The wind was always free. Most months we spent about twenty five dollars or less after we cleared Customs. When we were out in the ocean and lost the wind or it died, we would jump overboard and swim or clean the bottom of the boat until we got the wind again.

In the evenings Irene and I would play various card games or Dominos. She beat me at dominos and most of the time I won at cards. We also read a lot of books. When we were in a port with other sailors, we would trade books. It was not easy to find good books because most sailors liked dirty stuff.

When I would dive at a reef or around a coral head to shoot a fish or catch a lobster for dinner, hundreds or thousands of little fish would surround me and use me for protection from predators. They were so close and so many that I could feel them touch me all over. When I would go into the boat and look down all those little fish would look like a cloud, then like a flash they would be gone. There are so many interesting and exciting things to see on the ocean and in the ocean. Every day was a new day and new experience.

People asked me, weren't you afraid? My answer and favorite verse in the Bible is, Deu. 31:8, And the Lord, He it is who does go before you, He will be with you, He will not fail you, neither forsake you. Fear not, neither be dismayed. My favorite Christian song is: I can hardly walk without Him holding my hand. With that verse and that song there is nothing to be afraid of because He will always be with you. That is God's promise to those who love him.

We never got as far as we wanted to go. There were so many Islands that no one has been on for over two hundred years and we wanted to explore them. We would anchor off the Island, take our Dingy in and walk through the jungle. We would see old building, walls from old buildings without roofs and lots of wild life. Most of the wild life was the same as we have in South Florida.

After that I would dive and Irene would fish. All of our meat came from the ocean when we were out to sea. Irene is a very good cook and every meal when we had fish, the fish would taste different and very delicious. When Irene caught a fish for dinner, I would fillet or steak it, wash it in ocean water and she would put it in the fry pan. The sea water out in the ocean is very clear and clean. Some times when she would still fish with a rod and reel she could see fifty feet or more down and if a fish she didn't want got close to her bait, she would pull her line away from it.

At night depending on conditions, we sailed with only half of our sails up. In the morning after a half hour of exercise and a half hour of Bible study and prayer, I would put up full sails. Irene would fish and I would sit in the cockpit, turn on the autopilot and read the Bible or a good book. Most of the fish she caught were very good to eat and if we didn't need it she would let it go. Once she caught a ten foot shark. We cut the line at the shark's mouth and let it go. The hooks she used are made with cheap metal and will disintegrate in a few weeks or less. On one island that was not inhabited, we found a nice big Iguana. I wanted to kill it and have it for dinner but Irene talked me out of it. We ate alligator and it was very good but no iguana. One Island we stopped at was named High Borne Cay. No people lived on that island but it was full of Iguana. They were from a few inches long to full grown which is about six feet long.

When we needed fresh vegetables we would set sail to an inhabited island, buy some vegetables, visit with the people that lived on the Island and then set sail again. All the people we met on the islands were very nice, friendly and wanted to talk. Sometimes it was hard to get away from them. They wanted to know all about us and of course, we wanted to know all about them. Twice we took some young boys out to our boat in our dingy. They enjoyed it as much as we enjoyed taking them and visiting with them. Their English is a little different from ours so we had to really pay attention to understand them. The next morning we went ashore to walk and noticed about thirty children lined up in front of their school. Before they went in the Principle prayed and asked God's blessing on them and their studies. All the children said Amen. I told a teacher that was very nice. She said we always pray before school starts. I know you can't pray in the States and that is so sad because talking to God is very important and always helps. The name of that town is: Georgetown on The Great Exuma Island.

Most guide books and nautical charts are out of date because every storm changes the contour of the ocean floor. We tried to go into an island that was supposed to have two hundred people and a deep channel for the supply boat. When we got near we found the channel was no longer there and the few supplies they get are brought in on a small boat. Most of the people had moved off of the island. We anchored about a mile out and took our dingy in. Then we walked about two miles to the town and a store. When we arrived we found there was only one store and less than fifty people on the island. The store was nearly empty except for a big fat cat sitting on top of a box of corn flakes. The owner tried to shoo it away but it would not move so she picked it up and put it on the floor. The cat looked up at her as if to say, why did you wake me? We never saw any rats on the islands but I'm sure there are some or that cat would not have been that fat. We saw very few cats on the islands and the few dogs we saw looked skinny and sick. The people that live there don't have enough money to buy cat or dog food. There are lots of birds and some islands have a few chickens.

Most of the islands are made of volcanic stone and only very hardy bushes or trees will grow. Some islands have what they call pot hole farming. They dig a small hole in the volcanic stone and fill it with dirt and sand then plant a vegetable seed. Their peas and onions are very good but most food is brought in by government boat. On at least one island they grow onions. We were not on that island but they must have good ground. There is a big market for them because of their taste. One time we bought a box of mixed vegetables from the government warehouse. There were some onions in the box and they were very good. Years ago they grew cotton trees on some islands. When we would explore the uninhabited islands, we would often see some cotton trees still standing. They were about six feet tall.

On one island we met the Bush Doctor. It was a large island by the name of New Bight Cay. He was the only Medicine Man on the island. Once or twice a year a Nurse would visit the island. He told us about all the medicines he makes from leaves and roots. We spent about two hours talking to him. He sounded like a real Doctor and Scientist. He also showed us the large hard leaves they use instead of dinner plates and smaller hard leaves they use for fork and spoon. The people on the islands don't have much but they were happy, content, love the Lord and have a good church on some of the Islands. If they did not have a Church on their Island, they would get in a boat on Sunday and go to an Island that has a Church. We attended their churches several times on different Islands and enjoyed it very much. Their services last all day and sometimes into the night. They prayed, preached and sang a lot and at one or two o'clock they always had dinner at the church and asked us to join them. The food and fellowship was very good. Most of the meals we ate on the Islands were a type of pea or bean with rice and chicken, fish or shrimp. It all tasted very good and the people were always very friendly and happy. We will never forget them.

Another Island we visited was Little Exuma. There were only about twenty people on that Island. One was a little old Lady they called the Shark Lady. She would go on the ocean with her little boat, catch a shark, eat the meat and make beautiful jewelry from the bones. Irene bought something and asked the lady to make her a ring like the one she had on. Three days later we returned to get the ring she made. It was very beautiful, made from a Shark Bone with a nice Island Stone.

The sun sets were the most beautiful thing to see. Every night we would sit in the cockpit and watch the sunsets. It was better than any movie. They were always different. We never got tired of them. Night sailing was also different. When the moon was full, the sky was so clear you could read a newspaper and when there was no moon the stars were so near, you could almost touch them.

At night someone always had to be on watch in the cockpit because ships, fishing boats and barges are on the ocean. Most are on autopilot and the crew is either asleep or playing cards. You could see from a distance what type of boat it was because different kinds of boats or ships have different lights. For example, sailboats have one light on the top of the mask. The most dangerous vessel you had to watch for was the Tug Boat towing a Barge. There might be a cable one half mile to a mile long between the Barge and the Tug Boat. When it got dark I would have a strong cup of coffee and stand watch until midnight. Then I would wake Irene. She would make a little lunch and we would listen to a preaching and a Christian music tape or CD. Then I would go to bed in the cockpit and Irene would stand watch until it got light. When we saw a boat or ship at night we would call them on the radio to make sure we would not be too close or get a back-wash from their propeller that would rock our boat. We had two radios on our boat. One was a high frequency and the other very high frequency. Depending on the time of the day or night, we could talk to people around the world. Every boat at sea had to have a VHF radio for emergency and to talk to other boats nearby. The VHF radio is the radio that is monitored by the Coast Guard. Several times I heard them call all boats and tell them to be on a lookout for a certain boat missing or in trouble.

One day when we were sailing we had about a ten knot wind. We were going about four miles per hour. I was in the cockpit reading a book and Irene was below deck. A big wave about six feet high came from nowhere and hit us hard on the side. I grabbed the wheel to hang on and Irene was thrown around below deck and hurt her arm and leg. We watched the wave go rolling on and the ocean was smooth as glass. There was not a ship in site. Maybe it was an earthquake under the ocean. Any guess is good. We will never know, and then a few days later about mid-morning, we saw a large Whale. It looked fifty feet long and coming straight for us. It was about one half mile from us so we steered right and passed about two hundred feet apart. It is reported that Whales have tipped some sailboats over.

A few years later we were sailing in an area where the tide was very high and very low. I didn't have a tide chart for that area so I just guessed. When it was getting late in the day and we were close to shore we decided to anchor for the night and both go to bed. The water was twelve feet deep and I thought that was more than enough because we only needed four feet. We anchored and went to bed. When we woke up our boat was on its side. We looked out and found the nearest water was two hundred feet away. What a surprise! We got off our boat, walked around on the ocean floor without water and waited until the tide started to come in. When our boat was upright we set sail, a little smarter. Irene said: I told you to get a tide book! (She doesn't say much but when she does she is always right)

We met some very nice Sailors and a very few that were different. We made friends with a Doctor, a Dentist, a Lawyer and Retired

Members of the Military from upper enlisted to top officer ranks. Two couples were good Christians that we would have liked to sail with but our plans were different. On one trip we were sailing about four miles off shore when a lobster boat called us on the radio and said they would like to trade lobster for liquor. We told them we didn't drink and had no liquor on board. They were nice about it and said thanks anyway. Then one morning we were sailing out in the ocean and could see two other sailboats miles away. One called us and said they would trade breakfast cereal for liquor. We told them we had no liquor and they said unkind words to us and said they never heard of a sailor that didn't drink. Another time we were anchored in the bay of a very nice island. They had a grocery store, a hardware store, a water plant and a nice church. There were about twenty boats anchored in that bay that would spend the winter there. Every day they would go ashore and play games or have races with their sailing dingy. We also traded books to read and helped each other with repairs. On our second day there a sailboat came in and anchored very near to us. I asked him to move over about twenty five feet more from us so when the tide changed he would not swing into us. He got very upset because I asked him. He didn't move. The next day I wanted to be friends with him so I told him I would move over in case a wind came up. That is when I discovered he was a Retired Air Force Pilot and an Alcoholic. We moved about five hundred feet from him, stayed there ten days and really enjoyed the other sailors and the games. As we sailed we met other sailors from countries around the world. Some sailors had young children that they home schooled on board their boat. Those children were like fish.

As soon as school was over for the day they would jump in the ocean and play. At that anchorage there were three families that traveled together. Some of the children were teenagers and had their own dingy. After school they would pick up other children so they could swim and play together.

After sailing for several years Irene was getting very good with everything on our boat. So I told her that I was going to promote her from first mate to co-captain. She asked what she had to do as co-captain. I said she could go up the mask once a year and check everything up there. She said I'm happy to be first mate. When I had to go up and do the checking or repair, she would winch me up and when I was finished I would ask her to lower me down. Then she would say, do you promised to do the dishes and a dozen other things. All I could say is Yes,Yes. Let me down!! When I got on deck I always felt like throwing her in the ocean but I never did.

How did we get mail? We had a mail box at a mail forwarding service in the States. That address was also our permanent address. All of our mail went to that address and box. If we were traveling in our Airstream travel trailer or on the Boat, when we wanted our mail we would call that service and give them the address to send our mail to. Sometimes there was so much mail at a Port Post Office that it was hard for them to find ours. One sailing couple we met had their mail sent in a bright yellow envelope. That was a very good idea but too late for us. This was our last trip and we were on our way back to the States.

After sailing for seven years and both of us very near to our seventy's, we decided that although we had enjoyed it very much, had lots of fun and met a lot of nice people, it was time to do something different.

We sailed to Norfolk Virginia and put our boat up for sale. It normally takes a long time to sell a boat like ours. I advertised in the nationwide boat catalog. We planned to set sail and go up around the Statue of Liberty and come back and wait for a buyer to call. Before we left I put an ad in the local paper just to cover all bases. The next morning when the paper came out I got a call. He was interested in buying our boat. He arrived an hour later dressed in a business suit and tie. He liked our boat. The next day we took him and his wife out for a two hour sail and they fell in love with it. All large boats are documented not registered. They must be surveyed to sell them and to get insurance. Registered boats have numbers on the front side and documented boats have a name on the back or stern. The name of our boat was: (you guessed it) "QUEEN BEE". The survey took all day and it passed as if it were new. Then we talked price and agreed on one. I made all the arrangements for the transfer and he asked if we would take cash, green money. I pondered that for a moment. What is he saying, that is a lot of money. Then I said yes. I made arrangements with a local bank not knowing what to expect because that would be too much money to have on the boat or to carry around. The day of transfer Irene and I were in the Bank waiting for him. He drove up in a bright red convertible and again dressed in a business suit and tie. He stepped out of his car with a very large Macy's shopping bag with a towel on top. The bank president, Irene and I met him at the door and we all walked to the conference room. The bag was stuffed full with fifty and one hundred dollar bills. My eyes almost popped out and Irene's were big as saucers. He dumped it all on the big conference table and some fell on the floor. A cashier marked and counted all of it. It was the right amount and all good money. After we were finished I asked him what his profession is. He said he was a Plastic Surgeon and the money came from patients that paid in cash. He has been saving for a long time to buy a boat like ours. As Irene and I walked away from our baby, our home on the water, we were both silent and shed a few tears.

Chapter Thirty One

We heard there was good square dancing in Melbourne Florida and the beaches were nice. We loaded our Airstream travel trailer, went there and started a new life style. The square dancing was good with nice people. Two months later I was elected Vice President of the club and the next year President. The club was normal size for that area but with my new ideas the club grew by seventy five percent. When my year was up they wanted to elect me President for life but I said no, not even one year. It was time just to dance and have fun without the work.

A local newspaper reporter and photographer came to one of our dances and took pictures of Irene and me dancing. There was a two page article with pictures about us and square dancing. Then a local pizza place used some of the pictures for their advertising.

We found a good Baptist Church with nice friendly people and we got involved. I was an usher, a greeter, counted the offering, prayed and did other duties that the pastor asked me to do. In the afternoon we would go with another couple to a Nursing Home and hold a Service. We liked our new Church, both Pastors and all the people in the Church. We liked the area and decided to buy a home and stay there.

Chapter Thirty Two

The next year I took a job as Vice President of a Corporation and two years later the President retired and I took over as President. When I took the vice president job, Irene wanted something to do. The job of Postmistress for the Corporation was open so she took that job. She had three hundred mail boxes to work six days a week until I retired, then she also retired. The job as President of a Corporation was not the kind of work I was skilled at or liked. After leaving that job I really missed it the same as all the other jobs I ever had, but life goes on.

Chapter Thirty Three

We wanted to leave Florida in the summer so I could have a nice garden. I love good fresh fruits and vegetables. I tried to grow them in Florida but couldn't get any vegetables to grow where we lived. We drove through Georgia, South Carolina and Tennessee. We wanted a good church, nice home and a place for a vegetable and flower garden. We found it all in Anderson South Carolina. The Church here is one of the best we have ever been part of. Very friendly people with dynamic preaching and the best music I ever heard in any Church. We bought an attractive home on a half-acre of land with a nice vegetable and flower garden. We then sold our home in Florida. Now we spend the winter months in Florida in our Airstream Travel Trailer and the rest of the year in Anderson South Carolina.

Chapter Thirty Four

Sometimes people that know me will ask? If you could live your life over, what would you do differently? There are good times and bad times in every bodies life. We can't re-do the life we lived. Jesus was the only good and perfect person on earth and they killed him. We make a lot of mistakes as we go through life and most of us live through them. But to use a wish list or a wonder what if list, first; I wish that I could have gotten saved earlier in my life. Eight or ten years old would not be too young. Next; stayed with the girl in Moorhead Minnesota, finished school there and continued working in the Bakery. Next; know the girl in Kansas better that taught me to roller skate.

My advice to anyone would be: Have a strong "want to". Never slow down. Never give up. Be prepared for a detour. Be honest, Love, and forgive. Whatever kind of work you do, do it the best you can. And always ask for God's help. When you are saved, his spirit lives in you and he will always be there to help you.

I thank God for the faith in myself that He gave me, my ambition, my abilities, my talents and for my achievements. I'm 85 years old now, retired and still square dancing. I have the feeling of a full and very happy life with Irene, the love of my life, the wife that God had a hard time giving me because I thought I knew best.

Made in the USA
Charleston, SC
23 July 2016